Oral Language Across the Curriculum

Multilingual Matters

Bilingualism: Basic Principles (Second edition)
HUGO BAETENS BEARDSMORE
Evaluating Bilingual Education: A Canadian Case Study
MERRILL SWAIN and SHARON LAPKIN
Bilingual Children: Guidance for the Family
GEORGE SAUNDERS
Language Attitudes Among Arabic-French Bilinguals in Morocco
ABDELÂLI BENTAHILA
Conflict and Language Planning in Quebec
RICHARD Y. BOURHIS (ed.)
Bilingualism and Special Education
JIM CUMMINS
Bilingualism or Not: The Education of Minorities
TOVE SKUTNABB-KANGAS
Language Proficiency Assessment (Four volumes)
CHARLENE RIVERA (ed.)
Pluralism: Cultural Maintenance and Evolution
BRIAN BULLIVANT
The Education of Linguistic and Cultural Minorities in the OECD Countries
STACY CHURCHILL
Learner Language and Language Learning
CLAUS FAERCH, KIRSTEN HAASTRUP and ROBERT PHILLIPSON
Bilingual and Multicultural Education: Canadian Perspectives
STAN SHAPSON and VINCENT D'OYLEY (eds.)
Multiculturalism: The Changing Australian Paradigm
LOIS FOSTER and DAVID STOCKLEY
Language Acquisition of a Bilingual Child
ALVINO FANTINI
Modelling and Assessing Second Language Acquisition
KENNETH HYLTENSTAM and MANFRED PIENEMANN (eds.)
Aspects of Bilingualism in Wales
COLIN BAKER
Minority Education and Ethnic Survival
MICHAEL BYRAM
Age in Second Language Acquisition
BIRGIT HARLEY
Language in a Black Community
VIV EDWARDS
Language and Education in Multilingual Settings
BERNARD SPOLSKY (ed.)
Code-Mixing and Code Choice: A Hong Kong Case Study
JOHN GIBBONS
The Interdisciplinary Study of Urban Bilingualism in Brussels
ELS WITTE and HUGO BAETENS BEARDSMORE (eds.)
Introspection in Second Language Research
CLAUS FAERCH and GABRIELE KASPER (eds.)
Talk and Social Organisation
GRAHAM BUTTON and JOHN R.E. LEE (eds.)
Raising Children Bilingually: The Pre-School Years
LENORE ARNBERG
Perspectives on Marital Interaction
P. NOLLER and M.-A. FITZPATRICK

Oral Language Across the Curriculum

David Corson

MULTILINGUAL MATTERS LTD
Clevedon · Philadelphia

British Library Cataloguing in Publication Data

Corson, David
Oral language across the curriculum
——(Multilingual Matters).
1. Learning 2. Oral Communication
3. Communication in education
I. Title II Series
370,15′23 LB1060

Library of Congress Cataloging-in-Publication Data

Corson, David.
Oral language across the curriculum.

Bibliography: p.
Includes index.
1. Children--Language. 2. Oral communication.
3. Language arts--Correlation with content subjects.
I. Title.
LB1139.L3C645 1987 372.6 87–31512
ISBN 0–905028–97–X
ISBN 0–905028–96–1 (pbk)

Multilingual Matters Ltd,
Bank House, 8a Hill Road,
Clevedon, Avon BS21 7HH
England.

& 242 Cherry Street,
Philadelphia, PA 19106–1906,
U.S.A.

Cover designed by Jussi Nurmi.
Typeset by Photoprint, Torquay, Devon.
Printed and bound in Great Britain by
Short Run Press, Exeter, EX2 7LW.

for Pat, Tim and Beth

Contents

Preface

Because this book aims to fill a gap in the teacher education literature that exists in many countries, the terms used for "levels of schooling" are unlike those in use in any single country. I use "first school", "middle school", and "senior secondary school" to refer to the following age ranges and schooling types: *First School* covers the age range of two years to the end of the seventh year; it includes not just kindergartens, pre-schools and the junior primary or elementary grades, but playgroups, play-centres, child care agencies and day nurseries as well. *Middle School* covers the age range of eight years to the end of the thirteenth year; it includes the upper primary or elementary grades, the first two years of secondary, high or comprehensive school, or the entire range covered by most middle schools where they exist. *Senior Secondary School* covers the age range of fourteen years to the young adult; it includes the upper years of secondary, high or comprehensive school, and matriculation colleges, community colleges or sixth-form colleges in some systems. My choice of these terms is explained in greater detail in the relevant chapters. The interested reader is not advised to see these divisions as categorical ones: it is wrong to think that the material in any one section can be grasped without a rich acquaintance with material in the others.

This book is the result of reading, practical experience and reflection on mother tongue acquisition over the years 1981 to 1986. There are many who have contributed advice or assistance of a direct kind. I am especially grateful to students and teachers in schools in South Yorkshire, London, Wollongong, Sydney and Tasmania for their welcome and assistance. In particular, too, the assistance of people at Multilingual Matters is much appreciated.

David Corson
Massey University,
Palmerston North,
New Zealand.

1 Knowledge, thought and language across the curriculum

Language development is not something that we can understand in a piecemeal fashion. Although books can be written with chapters that divide children's language growth into sections separated by age, it is wrong to think that any one section can be grasped without a rich acquaintance with the others. Whether you are a teacher of the very young, a teacher of primary level children or of children in their senior years of schooling, there are good reasons for you to have a broad understanding of the processes of oral language development as they apply across the age stages.

Firstly, it is necessary for those who teach high school children to know how children's language has developed in the earlier years, since they will meet many children at high school level who remain, in some ways at least, at a stage of linguistic and intellectual development out of step with their classmates. It is just as necessary for infant teachers to know where children go in their language development after they leave the first school, since in many ways the teaching approaches that are used in the first school are designed to prepare children for the life and language activities that follow in later years. At the same time the middle school teacher, dealing mainly with children of primary age, needs to consider both the following questions: where have the children come from in their language, and where are they going. Both are essential factors in determining what the middle school teacher can or should do with students in the middle school.

A second reason for teachers to have knowledge in breadth about language development relates to the role of the "teaching profession" as it continues to change towards the end of the twentieth century. People have to be versatile if they are planning to be teachers these days; few teachers today can expect to spend all their teaching days only in a primary, infant or secondary school without meeting some teaching at one or more of the other levels. Nothing offers a better insight into the development and the interests of children, at every level, than a broad grasp of their linguistic development. Finally, on the same point, most teachers are parents sooner or later; there is no knowledge more useful and attractive to parents than a knowledge of the directions and potentials of their children's language.

This first chapter seeks to make the links between language and educational success plain: it suggests how thought is dependent upon language, how we manage to acquire and display our knowledge through language, and how important language is in helping human knowledge to grow. The place of language in the learning process is made clear, and this theme is carried forward to indicate why the doctrine of "language across the curriculum" has become so respected and enduring among educators.

In Chapter 2, "The case for oral language in schooling", the rationale for this book is presented. In that chapter I assemble the most compelling of the available arguments to suggest that more attention be given to oral language work in schooling than is presently the case. I draw upon evidence and authoritative views from the sociology of language, psycholinguistics, sociolinguistics, cognitive neuropsychology, anthropological linguistics, general linguistics and the philosophy of knowledge and the curriculum. The points assembled argue for instructional changes with a greater focus on oral language as an educational aim and as a pedagogy for learning.

Chapters 3, 4 and 5 provide the basic material, the background knowledge and a range of approaches to oral language work at the first school, the middle school and the senior secondary school levels. At each level I suggest that oral language serves a somewhat different function in the teaching and learning process: In the first school, concentration on oral language is very nearly the whole curriculum; it has the central place, not just as an approach to learning at this stage but also as the chief educational objective of the first school. In the middle school years, when the limits of future language potential may be determined for children in a near-final fashion, proficiency in oral language becomes a desirable attainment; at the same time, purposeful talk becomes a tool through which intellectual development can be accelerated: for upper primary and lower secondary children talk becomes a means for absorbing patterns of thinking that were previously not their own. In the senior secondary school the emphasis on talk should increase, if anything, since adolescents have a well-developed flair for learning through oral language: learning efficiency is likely to be enhanced by talk at this stage. "Discovering their own meanings" becomes an attractive orientation to learning for adolescents for related reasons: firstly, at this stage they are often less inclined to respect their teachers as authorities; and secondly, they often find that their own conjectures about the world are too complex and too personal for them to be refuted merely by the "teacher telling".

At each level I suggest that we need "experience-based talk". The meaning of this key phrase changes as it is applied across the age ranges and across the curriculum. As the child's ability to learn from experience varies and as those "experiences" themselves take on subtle variations, the place of talk in the process of schooling changes, although at no time is the close and inseparable bond between language, learning and education broken or even stretched.

Language and education

We know that children's differences in language ability, more than any other observable factor, affect their potential for success in schooling. It is only in the last two or three decades that educationists in general have felt it necessary to state a fact that earlier educationists regarded as too commonplace to warrant stating: that language is the central achievement necessary for success in schooling. It is clear that achievement in schools is highly dependent on the child's ability to "display" knowledge. This display almost always takes the form of spoken or written language. Child language will often be the first contact teachers have on which opinions of student potential can be based, while in the closing stages of schooling language contact through formal or informal assessments is often the only link between students and those assessors who finally declare a child's educational fate. Nor is it an artificial or improper matter that language on display is the central achievement for school success. A school curriculum is a selection of knowledge from the culture: all those things in the culture (or from other cultures) considered worth passing on through schooling. Since all forms of knowledge are "filtered" through language, the chief item of knowledge in any culture is its language. The chief object of the school is to encourage the complete mastery of the language of the culture, since without this mastery children are denied power and influence over their own affairs and an opportunity for success in education.

Yet there is far more to the link between language and education than even these important concerns. Education is concerned with the activities of "thinking", "knowing" and "learning". We have strong indications from studies in cognitive psychology and from studies in epistemology of the way language and thought, language and knowledge, language and the roots of the intellect are connected. I shall refer to the views of a number of well-known and complementary authorities in presenting the case for this point about the centrality to be given to language in education through its priority in the activities of thinking, knowing and learning.

Language and thought

First of all a warning: this subject is among the most difficult teachers may wrestle with, even if my treatment of it in this book is only introductory. It is certainly a most rewarding subject, though, for a dedicated teacher to be expert in. Its difficulty comes from the fact that in thinking and talking about "language and mind" we are using language to talk about language: that is, we are using an abstract thing (thought) to think about another abstract thing (language) in an abstract way (in some language); so it is three times "removed from reality". In what follows I will use concrete examples wherever I can, but I am mentioning all this now to provoke you into concentrating all your powers: browsing through these matters is likely to confuse rather than help understanding.

Bruner, writing as a cognitive psychologist, bases his views on the place of language in education upon empirical evidence, much of which he has been instrumental in discovering himself, and upon wide contacts with children in learning situations. In summary his early conclusions (1966) about the link between thinking and language are these:

1. Intellectual growth is characterized by increasing independence of response from the immediate nature of the stimulus, an independence made possible by the mediating role of language. To give an example: if young children are asked to talk or write about something, it is easier for them to do so if the subject matter is present in the context; older children are more able to draw on their greater resources of language to compensate for things that are missing in the present context; moreover, they are able to use that mediating language as a basis for further acts of language use.

2. Growth depends upon the development of an internal storage and information processing system that can describe reality. Again, an example: older children, describing something in the present which is absent, are only able to do so easily if they have acquired sets of meanings relating to that something; using their "storage system" they can attach names to these sets of meanings (the words and phrases of a

language) and further, they can make statements about these sets of meanings (using the infinite range of possible sentences made available to them by their grasp of the language's structure). As far as we know the only genetically endowed information storage system that humans have is a language-based one: this means that all the experience-based memories that we have are to a large extent encoded in some language system.

3. Intellectual development involves an increasing capacity to say what one has done and what one will do. An example: even though little children's memories may be filled with immediately past experience, they will be unable to tell you much about those experiences. Why? Because they lack the language to link up with those memories; to map onto the concepts and to organize their thought into sentences; they will also have difficulty telling you clearly about what they plan to do, for much the same reasons.

4. Systematic interactions between a tutor and a learner facilitate cognitive development. This speaks for itself: the "courtesy of conversation" in Bruner's view is part of the "courtesy of good teaching": we learn language by using language in the company of experienced language users to receive or to give messages.

In a later paper (1975) Bruner sets out his ideas on language as an instrument of thought. I present these ideas here, interpolated with views from elsewhere.

Bruner talks about three different kinds of "competence" that go together to make up "language proficiency". The first of these is that kind of "*linguistic competence*" which is regularly mentioned by writers in linguistics. Chomsky has long been associated with discussion on this "faculty". He contends (1979) that there is a "universal grammar" that is "a genetically determined property of the human species"; children do not learn or acquire this competence in any sense; rather they apply it in developing knowledge of language. Perhaps this complex idea can best be grasped by trying to imagine what knowledge of language would be left to us after the knowledge that we have of any single language is taken away. What remains is an innate readiness and capability for language, possessed by all members of our species because of that membership. Since it is something that education cannot affect or influence in any way, and since Chomsky's ideas on this matter remain very controversial in any case, this kind of competence need not concern us here.

The second kind of competence is "*communicative competence*", discussed in the writings of Hymes (1972). This competence includes the ability to make and understand utterances appropriate to the circumstances in which they are made. Speakers bring to a particular setting certain assumptions and expectations about when and how to speak and the sorts of things that can be said to particular people in particular situations. Romaine (1984) emphasizes that an individual's communicative competence can be greatly affected by variations in setting; for example, what children in school can do with language in the relative security of their own classrooms may be quite different from what they can or want to do in front of a school assembly. While Chomsky's idea of "competence" separates it from language "performance" (what we really do with our language), communicative competence accepts performance as an integral part of the language capability that children develop. Performance has its own underlying "competence" which is not fully "linguistic"; it is influenced by entities removed from our linguistic faculties — other cognitive systems, for example, including our expectations about three dimensional space, about texture and sensation, about human behaviour, inanimate objects etc. More than this, influences outside the mind may be crucial: a child might otherwise have a high degree of communicative competence in a given situation, yet still be prevented by illness or nervousness from displaying that competence in performance.

An important point is that Chomsky's "competence" is regarded by him as something that we all share to the same degree; it is in communicative competence where differences in language development show up, although, as Bruner points out, every normal person can be expected to achieve a communicative competence without special training. He says that this competence involves the ability to engage successfully in the "concrete operations" that Piaget and his associates describe (Piaget & Inhelder, 1958; Piaget, 1978). This second kind of competence is of central concern to teachers in infant and primary schools. As I shall suggest in Chapters 3 and 4, teachers in first and middle schools in particular have a key responsibility for promoting the development of children's communicative competence as fully as possible across a range of contexts, functions and styles of language.

The third kind of competence Bruner calls "*analytic competence*": this is a necessary acquisition for engaging in "formal operational reasoning" of the sort that begins to develop towards the end of the primary years and which is required from adolescents by the intellectual demands of the secondary school (see Chapter 5). This kind of competence is important not just in discussion about senior secondary schools; the foundations for analytic competence are laid in essential ways at earlier stages of schooling.

However, it is children's ability to reach a sophisticated development in their analytic competence that finally determines their educational fate. Bruner (1975:72) describes the workings of analytic competence as:

> "the prolonged operation of thought processes exclusively on linguistic representations, on propositional structures, accompanied by strategies of thought and problem-solving appropriate not to direct experience with objects and events but with ensembles of propositions."

In short, Bruner suggests that analytic competence is the ability to use language for thinking, a possession that is not acquired without exposure to some long-term educational process that integrates rich and complex interactional language activities.

The language and thought debate, which I am broaching in this section, is a vital and fascinating chapter in human intellectual history. Steiner (1978) believes that the most stimulating discussion on the relation between language and thinking is that between Vygotsky and Piaget. Since that debate in the 1930s Vygotsky's conclusion on this matter (1962) seems to have gained the upper hand, even while remaining very controversial. His view can be simply stated: thought and speech have different origins; in the *linguistic* growth of the child there is a pre-intellectual stage; correspondingly there is a pre-linguistic stage in *thought* development. It is when the two independent and different lines converge that thought becomes verbal and speech becomes rational. This convergence depends on outside factors: the child's exploration of the social aspects and the functions of language leads to the development of logic on which inner speech is based. For Vygotsky, then, verbal thought (thinking in language) is not an innate and natural form of behaviour; thinking in language is something determined by a historical-cultural process; we come to think in language partly because human cultures have found this a useful thing to do; and this kind of thought has specific properties and laws that cannot be found in either thought or speech on their own. Vygotsky (1962:148) concludes from his observations that the transition from inner to external speech (or vice versa) is not a simple translation from one language into another:

> "it is a complex, dynamic process involving the transformation of the predicative, idiomatic structure of inner speech into syntactically articulated speech intelligible to others."

Pondering these conclusions of Vygotsky's, Steiner puts all the products of human language into two categories: audible or voiced, and inaudible or unvoiced. In terms of quantity, there is every reason to believe that we speak inside and to ourselves far more than we speak outwardly to others. What has changed in recent centuries is the degree to which the diverse subject matters of internal speech have become acceptable subject matters for public discourse.

In explaining this Steiner says that "the contribution of women, of the young, of the economically and socially less advantaged levels of the community to the aggregate of enunciation, has sharply increased". This means that what once were intensely private matters (emotions, attitudes, values, fantasies, beliefs, etc.) are now freely spoken of; and in the speaking we change our inner speech about those matters in subtle ways. We have changed the way we think about things by talking about them. In this process of interaction we have come to understand many things that we would not have been able to puzzle out for ourselves as individuals in former times. Our knowledge about ourselves and about our world has increased immeasurably, simply because the taboos on talk have changed or fallen away: the shift in the balance of discourse (since about the seventeenth century) has been outward. This process in general has been a liberating one for humankind, promoting relatively open societies that are based on free speech and that encourage dialogue.

One thinker concerned with the links between language, thought and human freedom is the German social philosopher, Habermas. He uses the phrase "institutionalized discourse" to describe the change that has occurred in Western thought, largely since the Renaissance, that Steiner is pointing to as well. There has gradually developed a greater readiness to examine all kinds of issues in talk and to subject even our most firmly held views, prejudices and dogmas to criticism in language. Habermas (McCarthy, 1984) would like to see more of this; he believes, for example, that the problems of legitimacy that many Western social institutions face at present largely derive from a widespread failure to employ this critical discourse.

What others recommend, notably the philosopher, Popper, is the development and extension of that "critical tradition" first introduced by the pre-Socratic philosophers in ancient Ionia. This tradition demands a widespread willingness to challenge accepted dogmas and teachings in discussion. It is already certain, however, that out of our ever-growing engagement in critical discussion vast advances in knowledge have accrued: through this critical process the link between language and the growth of knowledge has become an increasingly dynamic one.

Language, knowledge and learning

There is a close connection between "knowledge" and "learning". Simply stated, learning is the acquisition of knowledge. In using the word "knowledge" we usually see it as a shorthand way of saying other things: for example, we usually mean "knowledge and understanding" when we say just "knowledge", since it means very little to have "knowledge" on its own: "knowledge" that is not available in some way to help us understand the world or operate within it. Also, in Education, we often use the word "knowledge" in a broad sense to include things like "skills" and "values". When we talk about children acquiring "knowledge" through education, we are usually implying that their understanding of the world has been improved in some way and that this often involves the learning of skills and the development of values or attitudes. In this section I am using "knowledge" in that broad sense.

Barnes, Britton & Torbe (1986) are three well-known figures in language and education theory development, even though interested in different aspects of that subject. They are in broad agreement, however, in their views on the links between language, learning and knowledge. In this section I present the views of these three theorists in outline; then, I focus on one of them in particular and show how that view of the relation between language and knowledge is very much in tune with an influential view in the philosophy of knowledge.

Torbe's central concern is with language management and the policies associated with "language across the curriculum". I give greater attention to these matters in the next section. He describes his stance on knowledge and learning as contrary to the orthodox view, which holds that we can judge that successful knowledge acquisition has taken place when the student has "got it right". He believes that those who see learning like that find it difficult to accept a very different model: a model of teaching and learning which values risk-taking, welcomes conjecture and sees error-making as inevitable and necessary. In brief, he concludes that all learners have to "discover for themselves".

Barnes' work will be referred to widely in the chapters that follow. His research, teaching and writing centre on "talk" as used by teachers and students in schools. From his studies he concludes that certain views on the nature of knowledge seem to be associated with corresponding views on the role of language in learning. In particular, he contrasts a "transmission" view of knowledge with an "interpretation" view: the former is concerned with the acquisition of information; the latter with cognitive and personal development. He sees the assumptions behind most approaches to teaching falling somewhere on a continuum between these two views, with the transmission view concerned mainly with the pupils' performance, and the interpretation view with their struggle to understand. These conclusions, and his research on problems related to them, have led Barnes to conclude that "talk" helps learning in any activity that goes beyond the rote and which requires understanding, especially the understanding of processes. For him, as for Torbe, all learning takes place through changes in the learner's existing model of the world.

Britton is interested in expressive writing and the use of talk activities as an aid in developing quality in written work. He believes that it is part of the nature of human learning that it proceeds by anticipation. We tackle a problem forearmed with alternative possible solutions. More than this, learners bring with them whatever they already know and interpret it in the light of new evidence. He suggests that it is through language that understanding develops in technical fields, since language brings our commonsense concepts to a point of engagement with the technical concept. Britton's ideas are shared by Barnes and Torbe. They also have much in common with current views in the philosophy of knowledge, views refined at length and stated most persuasively by Popper (1972), writing as a philosopher of science.

Popper's major interest has been epistemology, a field that considers questions like the following: How do we come to have knowledge; and what does knowledge consist of? For Popper it is only through *language* that deliberate criticism occurs, and this is necessary for the creation of knowledge. Here are the points that he offers to support this case:

1. a thought, once formulated in language, becomes an object outside ourselves: that is, a thought does not exist for anyone else but the thinker; once put into language, though, it becomes a real world event;
2. language is capable of criticism and therefore is part of the world of objective standards: that is, we can try to say when someone is *talking* nonsense but there is no point in trying to say someone is *thinking* nonsense, unless we have the evidence of that person's language to go on;
3. only thought contents that are expressed in some language can stand in logical relationship to one another, such as equivalence, deducibility or contradiction: that is, we can use the language of one another to find out whether things are so or not, and this creates new knowledge.

A point basic to Popper's view is that the creation of knowledge depends on a rich language framework and the possession of that framework by people; for Popper human thought and human language evolved together: language helps to explain the brain, the mind, human reason and freedom.

Perhaps the link between Popper's and Britton's views could be made plainer. For Britton, when expressive talk is used as a means of education, children bring their commonsense views, as anticipations, into the learning context and are asked to present them in language that is ready for reconciliation with more impersonal and objective public statements; for Popper, all knowledge grows through a process of conjecturing and refuting: we bring our commonsense theories or conjectures, as expectations about the world, to our problems and then proceed to eliminate error from those theories.

These views seem to me to overlap to a great degree. What Britton describes as a "learning method" in language work is an instance of what Popper proposes as his entire theory of knowledge: the most efficient way for human knowledge to grow, in Popper's process of conjecturing and refuting, is when our conjectures are made explicit in some language, because then they are available for criticism and improvement (along the lines suggested in 2 and 3 above). The task is to submit our theories to the most rigorous trial and error tests available, thereby eliminating their error as much as we can. In this way, at a personal level, our own knowledge grows; and more generally, in this way too, humankind's knowledge grows.

It does lend weight to educational theorists' views on the links between language, learning and knowledge to discover that those views match authoritative opinion from the philosophy of knowledge. With this expert support, the educational doctrine of "language across the curriculum", which I introduce in the next section, has met with little theoretical opposition. As I will explain, the practical problems for that doctrine do not derive from any lack of support by educators at a theoretical level.

Language across the curriculum

Many of the thinkers already mentioned in this chapter have been major contributors to the debate that ended in the doctrine of "language across the curriculum". The psychological thinkers of this century, who have been most interested in children's learning, have regularly approached their subject through considering language issues: Piaget, Vygotsky, Luria and Bruner are all noted antecedents of the doctrine who found rich implications for their work in the area of language. Added to these are those philosophers experienced in teaching children who derived from their experiences views about the links between language and learning: Wittgenstein and Popper both taught in Austrian schools and show the results of that practice in their writings. It is in the British school of curriculum theorists where the ideas of these and other thinkers began to come together. Notably, Moffett's book (1968) *Teaching the Universe of Discourse* set the scene for a new direction in curriculum matters as they relate to language and learning.

Moffett's key idea is that our ability to think depends on the many previous dialogues that we have taken part in. You will find this idea restated and paraphrased at various points in the chapters that follow, since it is the central rationale for this book. Language across the curriculum, as an idea, emphasizes the fact that we often fail to exploit students' language, especially their informal and expressive talk and writing, as a learning resource in the classroom. Fillion (1983) sets out the three basic tenets of language across the curriculum:

1. language develops primarily through its purposeful use;
2. learning often involves and occurs through talking and writing;
3. language use contributes to cognitive development.

These claims have been largely substantiated in the research work of many of the theorists cited in this book through their studies examining the observed behaviours of students and teachers. They provide the platform upon which a worldwide re-examination of the role of the student's own language use in their learning has taken place. *A Language for Life* (Department of Education and Science [DES] 1975), the report that resulted from a major educational enquiry in Britain, allotted a chapter to the doctrine, using the title "Language Across the Curriculum", thereby lending official support to a set of ideas which was already extremely influential in Europe, Australasia and North America. Perhaps the most advanced in its thinking on these matters, of all the world's education authorities, the Ontario Ministry of Education in Canada has adopted the doctrine as part of its public policy. Below is that policy cited in full (1984:7):

> *Language Across the Curriculum*
>
> Language plays a central role in learning. No matter what the subject area, students assimilate new concepts largely through language, that is, when they listen to and talk, read, and write about what they are learning and relate this to what they already

> know. Through speaking and writing, language is linked to the thinking process and is a manifestation of the thinking that is taking place. Thus, by explaining and expressing personal interpretations of new learnings in the various subject fields, students clarify and increase both their knowledge of the concepts in those fields and their understanding of the ways in which language is used in each.
>
> It follows, then, that schools should provide an environment in which students are encouraged to use language to explore concepts, solve problems, organize information, share discoveries, formulate hypotheses, and explain personal ideas. Students need frequent opportunities to interact in small group discussions that focus on the exploration of new concepts. In addition, they should be encouraged to keep journals in which they write thoughts, questions and speculations that reflect on their learning.
>
> Principals should provide leadership by encouraging all teachers to participate in developing and practising a school language policy, which is, in effect, a school learning policy. By allowing students to discuss and write in the language they already control, teachers can gain new insights into the difficulties that students are encountering in particular subject areas. In this way teachers can help students to avoid rote learning and to gain clear understandings.

The difficulties that arise in the task of bringing a policy of this kind into operation are many. I mention a major one of these at the end of this section and suggest how it can be overcome. Part of the difficulty for the doctrine of language across the curriculum is that its implementation requires major changes in teacher attitudes and in the choice of pedagogy that teachers make. You will find that this book is directly concerned with pointing to the attitude changes that are needed and with presenting pedagogical alternatives.

Some of the problems for language across the curriculum, though, can be eliminated by simply becoming clearer about what the doctrine means (French, 1985). Firstly, language across the curriculum is not solely or even especially a part of the responsibility of the teacher of English (or the teacher of any other mother tongue); it is the responsibility of every teacher at every level in important ways: it is a doctrine about learning, after all, and that is the central concern of education. Secondly, language across the curriculum is not much concerned with language as product, or with promoting language assessment in some way: its focus is on language as an instrument for learning, not performance in language (although some implications for performance will no doubt follow if the quality of learning through language is to be highlighted). Thirdly, language across the curriculum is not concerned with some or other "linguistic bias"; the enforcement of certain language styles or varieties is not an aim of the doctrine. An important teaching of *A Language for Life* is that teachers should place value upon the language that children bring to schools, and use that as a starting point for education, not as something to be changed or eliminated.

A great difficulty for "language across the curriculum" is suggested in the last paragraph of the Ontario policy above. Because language across the curriculum, by definition, cannot be the responsibility of any single teacher located at one point in the curriculum or in the age range, then by necessity responsibility for the doctrine shifts in a major way to the school executive: language across the curriculum becomes a function to be assumed by educational administrators as perhaps their central curricular concern in schools. My own interest in these matters is practical, since I teach Master's courses entitled *Language Policy Across the Curriculum* and *Fundamentals of Language Planning in Education* that are aimed directly at practising school administrators. Many topics and issues are relevant in designing school language policies. Maybin (1985) sets out some of these matters, in an introductory way, as they apply at primary school level. Marland (1977) gives a detailed and introductory treatment of secondary level language policy. A specimen policy, already in use in a school setting, is cited in Chapter 4.

There is much more that could be said about language policies, but they are matters that do not directly concern single teachers interested in promoting a use of oral language in their own teaching. The conclusion that should be derived from this chapter's discussion, however, is the central role played by oral language in all the recent thinking and in much of the practical action taken in modern approaches to schooling.

Summary

A good deal of schooling is devoted to "language on display"; the chief object of the school is to encourage mastery of the language of the culture. Humankind's efforts to understand the links between language and thought provide a difficult but fascinating debate. Development in thinking prowess depends on growth in language. Although language and thought are not identical, they develop together.

Teachers in first and middle schools have a key responsibility in promoting children's "communicative competence": this is our ability to make and understand utterances appropriate to the circumstances in which they are made. "Analytic competence" is the ability to use language for thinking. The building of analytic competence is a prime task of the school; foundations for this are laid in first and middle schools and judgements about its quality usually determine a child's educational fate.

Our capacity to think in language is not innate; as a species we have learned to do it. In recent times we have come to share the products of our inner thought more and more. This extension of talk into new areas has led to great increases in the growth of knowledge and a growth in human freedom. Learning takes place when we eliminate error from our existing conjectures about the world. For learning to be effective, language is necessary, because deliberate criticism occurs only through some language.

The three tenets of "language across the curriculum" are that language develops through its purposeful use; that learning often occurs through talking and writing; and that language contributes to cognitive growth.

2 A case for oral language in schooling[1]

As the main means of human communication, oral language recommends *itself* as a major focus of attention in schooling. Yet we know that oral language work is not given the attention it deserves in schools (Galton, 1980), even while teachers themselves acknowledge its importance and their willingness to do more (Bourke *et al.*, 1980). This chapter presents arguments for oral language work that go far beyond "the principal means of human communication" justification. It seems that a stronger case is needed than the commonsense attractiveness of recommendations in the British Newsom Report, *Half Our Future* (Ministry of Education, 1963):

> "Very high in this list we should place improvement in powers of speech: not simply improvement in the quality and clearness of enunciation . . . but a general extension of vocabulary, and with it, a surer command over the structures of spoken English and the expression of ideas."

More than a decade later the Bullock Report, *A Language for Life* (DES, 1975), devotes a chapter to the subject, "for we cannot emphasise too strongly our conviction of its importance in the education of the child". The Bullock Report renews the emphasis of Newsom by stressing that all schools must have, as a priority objective, "a commitment to the speech needs of their pupils and a serious study of the role of oral language in learning". This chapter assembles the points in a case for oral language work in schooling.

Oral language and success in schooling

Many educators are convinced that proficiency in oral language is essential for children to achieve their potential for success in schooling. As argued in Chapter 1, achievement in schools is highly dependent on the students' ability to express what they know clearly and in an accepted form, since the educational system is founded on the child being able to "display" knowledge. This "display" most often takes the form of spoken or written language. The child's oral language will often be the first contact the teacher has on which an opinion of the child's potential can be based. The quality of this display, the oral performance, can be used by teachers as an imprecise indicator of educational potential, especially if there are other indicators that reinforce teacher prejudices (such as children's dislike of schoolwork, lack of parental interest in the school, or evidence of disadvantage in the children's dress or appearance). Expectations can be adjusted accordingly. It is known that the teacher's expectations of children's potential can influence academic success, with children's true potential overlooked or reduced in effect. This view is especially supported by Rosenthal & Jacobson's 1968 study, *Pygmalion in the Classroom.* Verma & Bagley (1975) cite the "considerable amount of research" since *Pygmalion* that indicates that the average teacher has different perceptions and expectations of poor and minority group children, which lead to different treatment and depressed performances on the part of such children. The evidence of language is vital in confirming stereotypes and activating prejudices. The frequent presence, for example, of high-status Graeco-Latin words in the language of some school children will enhance the school reputations of those children. Their absence for other children may have the opposite effect (Corson, 1985: see Chapter Five).

What teachers are looking for in their students' oral language is the communication of "meanings". The richer and more diverse these meanings are, the more impressed will be the teacher. After the very earliest stages of schooling, when children have learned to structure their language, the chief factor that influences the communication of meanings is the content of the language: the use of words. By their choice and use of words, children can explain, describe, justify, and impress with their display of knowledge. Children often have greater resources of language, though, than their usual performances reveal. This can be a handicap, since in education it is what children do with these resources, how they are displayed, that matters. Although it is wrong for teachers to assume that the oral use of words on its own indicates cognitive prowess, in crowded classrooms this error in judgment does happen, especially when supported by the evidence of poor literacy attainment.

How will children learn to use language if they do not experience something to talk about that demands a rich use of language and if they do not have the opportunity to engage in that talk? Bruner (1980) reports findings in many societies where the main source of language learning is other children. Where talk between children is stifled, this source dries up. It is clear that words heard more often by young children are better organized and more easily recalled. The experience that really matters, however, is the very first tentative use of the word or phrase by children in their own speech. This is the experience that sets the notion into their repertoire of meanings, and this is the experience that provides the habit and motivation for further use of that concept. For the young child the experience and the word that names it unite when the word is used. For older children, when they use more abstract terms, the word itself is the experience. The meanings of abstract words, by definition, exist only in the minds of language users, not in concrete reality. The acquisition of these complex meanings is only achieved by children engaging in conversations that demand their use, since before the age of 15 it is difficult for children to acquire the meanings of complex words simply from their contexts (see Chapter 5). On the one hand, younger children acquire the key concepts of time, space, number, causality and classification from talking about their experiences (Tough, 1977). On the other hand, older children achieve key abstract conceptual learning, which is very necessary for later success in schooling, through oral language work.

There is evidence to confirm that a link exists between vocabulary power in children and their academic progress (Palmer, 1964). If vocabulary power itself depends on oral language experiences, as I have argued above, then the connection between the availability of oral language work in schooling and academic success becomes a more complete one. Other matters, very relevant to oral language and success in schooling, are dealt with in later sections. I now centre the discussion on examining the major link that concerns educational researchers: What is the cause-and-effect relationship between oral competence and literacy?

Oral language and literacy

Reading and writing both have their bases in oral language. The methods of using language in literacy are first established in oral competence, although there are functional differences in the everyday applications of the two modes (Goodman & Goodman, 1982). These points are clear, but there is an apparent confusion in the findings of researchers who look for evidence of a connection between oral proficiency and reading and writing proficiency. In longitudinal studies (Wells, 1974; Moon & Wells, 1979) at the University of Bristol, there are findings that connect oral language in the preschool years with later literacy development. Although preschool children's interests in literacy are not strong predictors of their knowledge of literacy on entering school, the quality of parental verbal interactions with preschool children is strongly predictive of the children's knowledge of literacy on entering school, which in turn is strongly predictive of attainments in reading by the same children at age seven years.

During the early years of formal schooling the link between oral language activity and literacy is less clear. One study (Gray *et al.*, 1980), which overviews previous research and reports its own new findings, claims it would be incorrect to assume that a cause-and-effect relationship between oral competence and literacy has been proven unequivocally. The study presents six pieces of research that support the claim that a strong link exists. Then the work of a number of researchers (including their own work), who report no significant link, is examined. The study concludes that a link is "not proven". However, closer inspection of all these studies reveals a clear difference in findings according to the ages of students assessed. Those studies that deal with preschool and kindergarten children (ages 4–6 years) report no significant connection. Studies that deal with older children and adolescents find that competence in oral language is essential for satisfactory performance in reading, in writing and in spelling. These discrepancies according to age need to be explained, because in the explanation lies a key to understanding the vital contribution that oral competency makes to literacy.

Children in their early years of schooling are confronted with a major problem for which they have had no prior experience: learning the mechanics of reading. There may be little transfer effect from oral language for these preliminaries to literacy, since the systems in the brain that produce and receive messages in words are to a large extent functionally separate for the oral and the written coding processes (Allport, 1983). Moreover, the speech centre in the brain and the centre controlling visual perception are separate (Popper & Eccles, 1977). For literacy learning, there may need to be a different and gradual integration of the functions of these two centres, with a new use of the pathways that connect the vision and speech areas, a use whose function is the decoding of abstract symbols rather than the perception and naming of objects and relationships in the environment.

Learning to talk is an easy and natural process for the child. Learning to read is hard work, since the language is filtered through skills that are not "language skills". Learning to read is also "unnatural" to the extent that young children's intellects at this stage are never fully exercised by what they read. Reading material never matches their already well-developed language ability in the sense that what they are able to read is limited by the mechanical skills of reading that they have been able to acquire. Their oral language use at this stage is far more advanced than the language of the books in which they are taught to read.

Putting together the information in the previous two paragraphs, we can see that the need for young children to learn the mechanics of reading is an important variable that confounds the link between oral language and literacy development. In comparing children's oral language in the early stages of schooling with their reading development and in looking for a link, researchers have been prone to overlook this intervening mechanical skill of "decoding symbols". This does not have much to do with the two language forms of speaking and reading, since learning to use this decoding function depends on factors that are for the child still somewhat independent of language, such as visual acuity. It is likely that a proficiency in oral language has no measurable transfer effect on the mechanical skills of reading. In the early school years, while these skills remain only partially mastered, transfer benefits are blocked and oral language can have little effect on literacy. Once they are mastered, however, that barrier falls away: oral language proficiency begins to promote literacy proficiency.

How does oral language development influence literacy development? A clue to the process exists once again in Vygotsky's work (1962) investigating the problem of the unequal development that exists in school children's oral and written language. Vygotsky concludes that it is the abstract quality of written language that is the main stumbling block. Children have little motivation to learn writing when we begin to teach it since they have only a vague idea of its usefulness. Research in Scotland by Reid (1966) and in England by Downing (1969) confirms that reading is a mysterious activity for beginners. They have only a vague expectancy of what the activity consists in, its purpose and use. There is a "cognitive confusion", which Vernon (1957) found to be the chief symptom of reading retardation in older pupils. Many poor readers have had little experience of language being used to represent something absent in the present. Their experience of this *representational function* of language has been so limited that, when they meet the language of literary (which is the purest form of the representational function of language at work), they experience confusion in understanding what it is all about.

Appreciation of the representational function of language is gained prior to literacy by children being read to widely and frequently. Listening to the radio with concentration also sharpens an appreciation of this function. Experience in putting the function to work, for the preliterate child, can come only from using it in oral language. This asks children to make an oral representation of their own thinking, of things that otherwise would remain unexpressed. Language forms (words, tenses, moods, hypotheticals) that touch on the abstract must be tried out in speech to see how things absent can be represented in the present. This asks for a use of words and structures quite different from those needed in everyday talk about concrete events and experiences. It requires using language that attempts to make everything explicit, as does the language of literacy, and that communicates feelings, opinions, hopes, fears, theories and explanations. Without a developing facility in using the representational function of oral language to match their developing educational needs in literacy, children may fail to see the point of the latter, they may fail to identify with its words and structures, and may remain semi-literate as a result.

Other things being equal (such as the provision of a rich atmosphere of language experience and regular access to "oral literature" of quality) there are two supplementary ways of bridging the gap between oral language and literacy in order to allow one to promote the other. Teachers can either change the books that children read so that they are closer in form and function to the speech of beginning readers, or they can extend the forms and functions of children's oral language to suit the needs of literacy. Both approaches can be employed successfully if the developmental needs of children are taken into account. For beginning readers, whether young children or late starters, the language to be read can reflect the home background, the cultural and subcultural experiences of the beginning readers themselves; the language to be read will be the printed or written form of the language the children already know, perhaps orally composed by the children themselves. But this material will remain relatively concrete as long as the oral language on which it is based is itself divorced from the abstract and the representational. If children are to branch into reading materials that require higher levels of literacy (as they must as schooling proceeds) they must learn to use orally those forms and functions that appear in that reading material. Where children's own language background denies them oral language experiences to suit this extension, then the school's task, in giving them literacy, involves giving them new forms and functions in oral language as a prerequisite. Such a conclusion seems inevitable. Anastasiow (1979) reports research that links literacy and oral language levels in a correlational relationship that suggests direct cause and effect. The words children use in their own speech are easier to read in print than words they do not use; the richness of the child's spoken language is related to reading success; deficient readers are deficient in oral language; and speech defects are related to reading problems.

Oral language, intelligence and problem solving

For Bruner, one of the crucial ways a culture aids intellectual growth is by the internalization of dialogue in thought. This prompts him to conclude that "the courtesy of conversation may be the major ingredient in the courtesy of teaching" (1972:123). Numerous studies of children who have spent long years in institutions show that lack of dialogue in the early years impairs language development and personality development. Preschools for the deaf are now an important part of the structure of education for the deaf because it is known that children with impaired hearing may suffer difficulties similar to normal children deprived of early language contacts. Britton (1970) goes further, inferring that intelligence itself, the ability to solve problems and cope with the world, is largely dependent on talk in early childhood. The connection he sees is a straightforward one: external speech, or dialogue, becomes internal speech, or thought, which operates to assist the solving of problems.

Barnes (1976) gives a concise report of research into speech and problem solving. A synopsis of that report presented here will make the connection clear. One study finds that adolescent boys more readily solve physical manipulation problems if they are asked to explain their moves while they are making them (Gagne & Smith, 1962). Another study reports that adult subjects more readily locate errors in the course of a computation if they are asked to put into words the ways errors could have occurred (Marks, 1951). A third study suggests that children's ability to put principles into oral language is closely related to the ability to reverse an operational process and play the role of "the other" (Lunzer, 1968).

Although speech is not identical with thought, it does provide the means of reflecting upon thought processes and controlling them, which is essential for exercising intelligence and for problem solving. It is possible to take this conclusion further and restate Moffett's conclusion that the ability to think depends on the many previous dialogues people have taken part in.

Oral language and thinking

There is little point in looking for research evidence that will confirm the effect oral language experience has on thinking. Because thinking is a mental act, it frustrates attempts by researchers to describe its processes with any degree of certainty. What we can do is make statements on which there is reasonable agreement and use these to infer a connection between oral language and thinking. This discussion extends the section "Language and Thought" from Chapter 1.

"If thinking can be said to be in anything at all" says the philosopher of education, Paul Hirst (1974:70), "then at times it would certainly seem to be in words." Introspection urges me to agree with this judgement. Certainly in order to have an understanding of what "analytic competence" might be, we need to recognize this simple claim: verbal thought is supported by words. I have already shown in an earlier section that oral language work promotes key conceptual learning: the acquisition of "word meanings". It follows, then, that oral language experiences can provide the raw materials at least for that form of thought that is "in words". A great many words in any language, perhaps the majority, have meanings that are "created" by the culture: meanings that do not refer to things we can sense. These abstract words are necessary for us to use when speaking about precise, culturally relative subjects. We also have to use them for thinking in those areas, since without the unity of thought that the words provide, the notions that the words name are ephemeral. When we lack the words, to that extent our thinking in those areas is probably less co-ordinated, more tied to the concrete, and less complex. For example, it may be impossible to consider the difference that exists between the notions named by the words "analysis" and "synthesis" if the thinker does not already "have" the words. If certain abstract words are lacking in a person's "thought vocabulary", then precise thought in the abstract areas those words suggest is difficult and perhaps often impossible. Only through hearing and trying out words in dialogue do young children acquire the words necessary for engaging in abstract thought, since conceptual learning from the nonverbal context is not easily achieved by children younger than 15 years (Peel & de Silva, 1972).

"There is a sense in which we do not really know what we think about anything until we have had to state it explicitly," says another philosopher of education, Richard Peters (1967:20–21); he recommends "not courses but conversation" as the means of bringing about an integrated outlook. Oral language used in effective talk, in external dialogue, is a rehearsal for later internal dialogues. I mean by this a rehearsal of manoeuvres, not a rehearsal of content; this is a personal contribution that we make to the development of our own "analytic competence". Moffett (1968) traces the course of dialogue where speakers take up statements that have gone before and develop them, adding conditions, suggesting a cause or result, negating, reformulating and qualifying. Out of discussions of this kind comes the ability to think without the support of other participants in dialogue. It is not just the subject matter for thought that oral language provides but the patterns of thinking, the analytic competence: the habit and the motivation to think in ways modelled on experiences of external dialogue, ways that develop as a result of those experiences.

Oral language and the "hypothetical mode of learning"

A great deal of rote learning confronts children in schools: learning strings of facts and formulas. Teachers know there is a lot of objective knowledge that has to be learned as quickly as possible. There is other "knowledge", though, about which we are less certain: for example, ethical and aesthetic values; these are things that cannot be acquired by rote learning. There are also "principles of procedure" in acquiring knowledge, sometimes called "processes", which cannot be taught directly but still need to be learned. To acquire this other "knowledge" and these processes, children need to be encouraged to discover their own meanings. Language makes knowledge and processes readily available for introspection, revision and reformulation. "Learning by talking" becomes a reality when those talking are encouraged to set up hypotheses in their talk, to verbalize doubt and not find the state of doubt intolerable (Rosen & Rosen, 1973). In this situation, provided children have been presented with a suitable problem that they are to attempt to solve by discussing it until possible solutions appear, the "hypothetical mode of learning" is in use.

The value of talking a difficult matter over with someone becomes apparent to most people at crucial stages of their lives (Barnes, 1976). In this form of oral language use, possibilities are tried out, ideas are attended to, evidence is introduced, and tentative decisions are reached. Learning proceeds. The context of the talk encourages a form of speech that is different from the more careful language of other situations; there are corrections of self and hesitations, changes of direction, and groping toward meaning that are characteristic of "thinking aloud". Hypothetical tenses, moods and abstract words appear in such talk, since these keep the subject "open". Oral language is the medium for employing the hypothetical mode of learning (Tough, 1979). There is no better way to encourage the learner to take responsibility for formulating explanatory hypotheses and evaluating them, activities essential for response in particular areas of the curriculum, such as literature, history, geography and social science, and for the creative thinking needed in mathematics and science.

In Chapter 1 I mentioned one of Vygotsky's major theories: his idea about inner speech and the changes that occur in the way children use language as they grow older. A second idea of Vygotsky's (1962) has received less attention in education but is now regarded as his most notable contribution to modern developmental psychology. This is his hypothesis about the "zone of proximal development": the difference between what individual children can do on their own in solving problems and what they can do with an adult's help. The more children are ready and able to take advantage of an adult's support in solving problems, the better the outlook for their future intellectual development. Vygotsky argued that the zone is a powerful influence on the child's future development. Adult skill and sensitivity in organizing oral language experiences are central to extending this "zone of development".

Oral language, self, and others: The real world

Oral language is closely linked with personality growth. How people speak identifies them as individuals. It is the most critical way in which individuals project and defend self in relation to others. Children whose oral language is under-developed are at a disadvantage in every kind of personal relationship, private and public. They fail to develop their full personal potential through lack of contact with others, and their own distinctive personal character is subdued. Children leaving school behind, who are not confident in using "talk" in all the major settings that life is likely to cast them into, will unavoidably fail to project themselves adequately in those settings. This can be an insurmountable obstacle for young people thrown into a job market, for example, where personal worth is very often measured by "first impressions": inexperienced young adults can easily miss the point and blame themselves for a failing that could so easily have been remedied by the natural use of "talk" as a pedagogy in their schools. Worse than this (for those around them), their lack of a voice in society can pose a threat to that society.

Perhaps the chief argument in the case for oral language work in schooling resides in the obvious fact that by its very nature oral language brings the self to others. One of the strengths of extensive oral language work is that it regularly confronts learners with viewpoints different from their own. They come to see that there are many problems for which there is no one correct solution. An openness to the world and others develops, founded on a recognition of the worth of the points of view of others and of others themselves. Yet even this is a service to the self. It leads to the development of critical thinking and analytic competence, as Peters (1967:19–20) argues: "Given that critical thought about the assumptions in which we are nurtured rather goes against the grain, it will only develop if we keep critical company so that a critic is incorporated within our own consciousness. The dialogue within is a reflection of the dialogue without."

A pedagogy across the curriculum

If the case for oral language is such a compelling one, why does it remain so understressed in the world's schools? The reasons for this are complex ones. They do need to be addressed if changes in direction are to be advocated and followed. There are many obvious factors operating against a use of dialogue in education, such as problems of class size, teachers' feelings of inadequacy in oral activities, the apparent inappropriateness of oral language subject matter, and the relative absence of effective pre-service training in this area. Teacher education institutions and those administrations engaged in selecting beginning teachers bear much of the responsibility for the present underdeveloped state of oral language work. However, even the practices of these organizations simply reflect deeper reasons. It is necessary to turn to the sociology of knowledge and the curriculum in order to offer deeper explanations.

Much of the work of schools is directed towards preparing children to succeed in higher levels of schooling. Curricula become increasingly more academic the closer children come to the end of schooling. Very often that endpoint is marked by an academically oriented series of examinations or other assessments that focus on the academic curriculum followed. Academic curricula pay high regard to what Young (1971) calls "high status" knowledge. They tend to be "abstract, highly literate, individualistic and unrelated to non-school knowledge". Young also suggests the contrasting conditions under which non-academic curricula will be organized: "oral presentation, group activity and assessment, concreteness of the knowledge involved and its relatedness to non-school knowledge". It is easy to see from these attributes which style of curriculum is more readily adapted to a use of oral language work and why formal schooling, as presently structured, lays less and less emphasis on oral language work the closer students get to their final years in school. It is also clear, though, that the curricula of first and middle schools lend themselves very readily to a wide use of oral language work since they are regularly non-academic in content and can display the organizational features that Young identifies. That they do not make a wide use of oral language work seems a result of teachers' dispositions and habits, picked up in their own schooling and training, not a result of lack of opportunity. Furthermore, as I argue in

Chapter 5, the positive influence of talk on effective learning probably increases for adolescents in the senior school. What I am advocating here, then, to teachers at every level, is not the artificial incorporation of oral language as yet another subject of the curriculum but its use as an indispensable learning tool: a pedagogy across the curriculum.

As mentioned in Chapter 1, a curriculum is a selection of knowledge from the culture: all those things in the culture (or from other cultures) considered worth passing on through schooling. The chief item of knowledge in any culture is its language. The chief object of the school is to encourage the complete mastery of the language, since without this mastery children are denied power and influence over their own affairs, and an opportunity for success in education. So language is both the content of the curriculum and its major objective. Clearly, it is also the major pedagogy for presenting a curriculum, whether that presentation be through the language of literacy or through oral language. My discussion in this chapter indicates the importance of oral language in schooling, recommending it as both objective and content. Literacy is also objective and content in schooling, but neither will the objective of literacy be served nor the content of literacy be presented if literacy is not also a major pedagogy in the school curriculum. If oral language is to be the objective and content in schooling, then, like literacy, it also needs to be a major pedagogy in the school curriculum. A curriculum without talk is stripped of a key pedagogy no less than a curriculum without writing.

At all levels of schooling, teachers need to see oral language work as a contribution to effective learning, not as something to be assessed in performance. They need to place value on the oral contributions of children in order to provide motivation in the talking context. They need to move away from centre stage more often and become listeners. As I mention in the chapters that follow, in the early stages of the elementary school, apart from listening to children, teachers need to give them something real to talk about, to make time for conversation and dialogue, and to develop an atmosphere of trust and respect that encourages talk. Teachers of very young children often do this as a matter of course, since for much of children's first school experience oral language *is* the curriculum. As children age and the curriculum of the school becomes more formal, deliberate strategies are available. Whatever the subject area, there is room for talk through which pupils can solve their own practical problems or come to terms with complicated ideas. Group discussion is the most favoured approach, focusing on manipulable materials with younger children and on issues and questions using work cards with older children. Improvisation work (plays without scripts), prepared by children in group discussion, is an approach to learning within subjects. It can provide vicarious representations of events and activities that cannot be brought into the classroom in any other way. Similarly, role play work fosters insight and learning in all those subjects where "values" are principal considerations. Role play equips children with a three-dimensional basis for "getting inside" the issue, as participants or audience, and for informing later discussion. Telling and retelling stories is a significant element in everyday communication. It has a place across the curriculum, and, like role play, improvisation or group discussion, can be a precursor to written work. I outline approaches to these and other activities in later chapters, indicating variations in their use that are appropriate at different levels, depending on the needs of the curriculum or whether it is communicative competence or analytic competence that the teacher wishes to promote.

Oral work not only leads to new learning; as a technique of revision it also reinforces the initial learning and prevents it from slipping away. Oral work can be used as an evaluation of pupil progress when teachers intervene in group talk and become consultants. It can precede any subject matter to reveal students' levels, interests and expectations, putting teachers in touch with the reality of their pupils (Freire, 1972).

Summary

There are areas of performance in schooling where we can be certain that oral language proficiency is a key factor in deciding success or failure. Oral language development is linked to achievement levels in literacy work, in problem-solving, in social skills and in the processes of learning and thinking themselves. That oral language work continues to be largely overlooked in modern schools is due to many factors. An examination of key tenets in the sociology of knowledge and the curriculum yields some explanation. There are specific strategies available for incorporating oral language work across the curriculum and as a chief pedagogy for promoting learning.

Note to Chapter 2

1. Reprinted from *Elementary School Journal*, 1984, 84, 458–67. The University of Chicago Press. All rights reserved.

3 Oral language in the first school

For much of children's first school experience, oral language *is* the curriculum. Apart from their physical and emotional well-being, nothing is more important to their education in these years than their oral language development. Their physical and emotional well-being itself may largely depend on that development. In earlier chapters I have already shown the important links that exist between oral language and thinking; between oral language and the acquisition of knowledge; and between oral language and educational success. This chapter provides the basic material, the background knowledge and a range of approaches, which the teacher can use to foster children's oral language at this level. In covering the age range of two years to the end of the seventh year, it is clear that this chapter is written not just for the teacher in a "school". Comments and suggestions are directed towards adults running play-groups, play-centres, school nurseries, day nurseries, child-minding centres, as well as teachers in kindergartens, pre-schools and the junior primary grades.

After presenting in outline a little of what we know about the process of early language acquisition and development, this chapter discusses the teacher's role in oral language work, matters of classroom organization and the central place oral work holds in all the areas of the first school "curriculum". A stress is laid on approaches and activities that are known to "work" in ordinary classes for ordinary first schoolers.

Early language acquisition and development

This vast topic does not meet with a full coverage here. Readers with more specialist or deeper interests will find comprehensive treatment of the subject in de Villiers & de Villiers (1978), Dale (1976), Romaine (1984), and Fletcher & Garman (1985).

In acquiring their language children perform one of the major feats of child development. For ordinary children this acquisition of language follows regular stages. These predictable stages through which the child proceeds are cross-culturally similar. This means that for all children in all societies there is a near inevitability in language acquisition in the early years, which is only hampered by the grossest forms of deprivation or by severe physical or mental handicap. Because all children progress regularly in language acquisition, attention has been given to the idea that there may be a *critical period* for this development (de Villiers & de Villiers, 1978). It is suggested that because of the biological nature of human beings language acquisition is a form of "growth", similar to other growing spurts which all humans pass through as they mature. It is further suggested that there may be a period of growth during which language is less readily acquired.

The beginning point for this period comes with the onset of babbling by babies. Even deaf babies babble at the same time as normal babies, although this ceases for deaf babies soon afterwards because they do not hear the feedback of their own sound. The end point for the period comes at puberty when the learning of language, either aspects of the mother tongue or other languages, seems to be more difficult for most people.

We can describe children's first words as the early *content* of their language. By two years they have passed through the beginning stages of experimenting with the production and modification of sounds. Using the lips, the tongue, the vocal cords and the body muscles, they control the intake and exhalation of air. They have begun the process of selection which leads them to focus the attention of their language on some of the many words which they encounter. They use features in their environment such as size, shape, change and their own influence over these things, to select "meanings" which are important to them. To these meanings a name is allotted: a word. Anyone familiar with the first words used by children will know that the meanings they attach to them may be much wider or much narrower than the meanings adults intend when using the same words. The meanings may also be entirely different from adult meanings, but by using the words and hearing them used in reply by adults young children learn to make their meanings more like the adult pattern. By adding new words they add new meanings. At the same time they refine the meanings of older ones as the content of their language expands. Every new word acquired "elbows its way in"; in this process it slightly changes the meanings of other words that are near to it in meaning.

Here are three examples of what Beth, a two year old, can do with words. They show the linguistic versatility and the creativeness of young children; they also suggest what an extensive process of learning language acquisition is and give some pointers for classroom practice at any age:

Beth had a toy "double decker bus", a phrase which she knew well. One day when she saw an ordinary bus in the street she exclaimed "there's a single double decker bus!" This is an example of the child very sensibly creating her own class of things, with the prime unit in the class being quite reasonably the unit with which she is most familiar (double decker buses); for Beth any variations in units in the class naturally preserve *all* the features of the prime unit and then add their own special features ("single"). I am dwelling on this example because what Beth is up to here is what we all get up to when we create new classes of things for ourselves: We begin by building the classes around the most familiar example of the class that we already possess, even if that example is not the most typical one. For instance, suppose that I am a person who has only ever encountered one kind of "dog" in my life, and I know that that animal is called a "chow"; if I am otherwise without the word "dog", I will perhaps generalize using the word "chow" to describe all other kinds of dogs that I encounter, whether they be big dogs, little dogs, barking dogs or sleeping dogs. They will all be varieties of "chow" to me, probably with some qualifying word used as in "single double decker bus" (Brown, 1959). You can see that this is a rather important insight for teachers to have into the way the mind works. It is plain that we start with the familiar, even if the familiar is a complex variation on the "natural" prime unit in the class and is therefore relatively unfamiliar to most other people.

Beth was looking forward to a family visit to Italy. Before the trip she heard her parents talking about going to a nearby restaurant; they were debating whether or not the restaurant would be open on Sunday. Joining in the conversation, perhaps in the hope of clarifying her own vague notion of what "Italy" might be, she asked: "Will Italy be open on Sunday?". What can this tell us about a two year old's language? Even after returning from Italy she might still ask the same question; it is not just a lack of experience of "Italy" that is causing this delightful confusion. It is more a lack of a class notion, such as the one that we attach to the term "country". But she will need many more real and vicarious experiences of "countries" before she will be able to sort herself out; before she can tell herself why it is not reasonable to believe that countries might "close for the weekend". Again, there is a pointer here for the connection between language and the intellect: When we acquire words they are not much use to us unless they can be placed in one or more *semantic fields.* Words have meanings partly as a result of the contrasts that they create with other words in their semantic fields. Much of the task of word learning involves understanding the associations with other words that new words have.

Finally Beth was enjoying a party with other children. She was asked to share some of her cake with her cousin but she refused saying: "I'm going to share this all by myself". Now we can conclude from this that Beth has missed the main point of the meaning of the word "share". In fact like so many words that adults give to children this word is only a "ritual" word for Beth. My point in presenting this example is to highlight the fact that children at this age are very good imitators. They can parrot back to us just about anything and we can convince ourselves that we have really equipped them with the meaning of a word rather than just a single part of the word's meaning, and perhaps not a very important part even.

I now want to look at some other features of early language development. Children acquire the "sounds" of their language in an approximately regular pattern of development. They begin by ignoring and discarding those sounds which have no function in the native language. Other sounds become dominant and are attended to because they mark changes in meaning. There seem to be critical periods in the acquisition and use of many of the sounds of English. The critical period theory may hold true for this aspect of language acquisition, since environmental influence does not affect the onset of babbling. Also, by puberty, the more general aspects of a child's accent are almost beyond changing. If certain combinations of sounds in the words of a language are not acquired early by children, it is likely that they will experience difficulty in using and even remembering words which include them.

We might describe the children's learning of the grammatical rules of their language as the acquisition of the language's *structure*. By two years they are using two word sentences. By three years most children have gained a remarkable proficiency in structuring their language. They are very versatile in improvising sentences to present their meanings with good effect, even when they are unable to use the most efficient sentence structures that might be available to adults for the purpose; for example, I have heard three year olds, in a range of contexts, use an active structure such as the following: "I didn't see anyone spill milk on the table", rather than the passive "I didn't see milk spilled on the table".

A familiar feature in the language of early childhood occurs in the speech of children from two years until eight years at least. Again Beth provides an example of this feature of "*the virtuous error*" at work:

Beth acquired the first person singular pronoun "I" at about the same time that most children do. After all there is one central person in the world for two year olds, so the word "I" can come rather early. When asked on one occasion to give some of her cake to her brother she cried: "Let I eat it myself". Now this is a "virtuous error" because the child is applying a language rule that she has "learned" (the subject of a verb goes in the nominative case), but it is an error all the same because her main verb is "let". These are mistakes that some teachers make a ritual of correcting; but it is a rather futile process because even well educated adults say "between you and I" when the convention specifies "between you and me". The important point is that there is little to be gained in correcting errors of this kind in the oral language of two year olds, five year olds or even twelve year olds. As a recommendation I suggest that teachers correct "virtuous errors" in older children's written language, and leave it at that.

Here is another "virtuous error", this time in adding an inflection to a word. Beth knew the word "long" and could pronounce it properly. On one occasion she was asking for something to be given back to her by her brother. She said: "Don't keep it any long-er" (not "long-ger"). She is demonstrating here a fine grasp of the rule for making an adjective into a comparative adjective by adding the inflection "er"; but she has not learned that words in "-ong" change their final sound before adding the inflection. How can we deal with this? Teachers could spend most of their days correcting errors of this kind with children in school! My suggestion is this: avoid correcting; simply find a way to repeat the word the right way, immediately after the child has used it wrongly. The teacher's model is a most powerful form of learning, whether learning good things or bad.

Grammatical structure, very similar to that used by adults, has been acquired by four years. It is a striking fact that children have little difficulty in acquiring any of the common structures of language. It is remarkable that even those deaf children who use a signing system and have not been taught rules of structure in this system begin to structure their language without any apparent assistance. This again lends support to the critical period theory. All children seem to use with ease rules for combining words into sentences, inflections and the infinite number of meanings which sentences express. By three years children use complete sentences, at least some of the time (Hendrick, 1975). By four years, they are able to give connected accounts of recent experiences. In following the language of others they are able to carry out activities at least as complex as following a sequence of two simple directions. By five years they can carry on a conversation, if the vocabulary is within their experience. They can use most pronouns correctly and apply the patterns of grammar used by the family and neighbourhood adults. Between five and seven years their vocabulary increases as contact with other children their own age increases. By seven they have mastered all the often-used grammatical rules, including irregular past tenses and agreements (Tough, 1979). They delight in trying out new words, even though they may not always get their tongues around them.

All of these skills the ordinary child acquires without much apparent difficulty. On the contrary, there is an ease and pleasure evident in the mastering, which masks the complex nature of this astonishing process. We still know relatively little about what is going on inside the child to promote this acquisition. There are a number of important things we can say, with some confidence, about influences external to the child. It is certain that the verbal exchange between parent and child plays a role of importance in assisting development. But there is not much *imitation* going on here (Cazden, 1972; Dale, 1976). Certainly, in structuring their language, children determine their sentences as a result of *their own* grammar, not the grammar of adults that they are later to master. Children make use of the language of other people as examples of language to learn from, not as samples of language to learn. Without conscious effort children organize their language learning in their own way. This depends on such things as who they are, how they see themselves in relation to others, and who they want to be. While imitation plays only a slight role, so too does adult *correction* have little effect. It seems that language is acquired and develops through the child *trying to use* language. As well as learning by talking, young children learn to talk by talking. All they seem to need is someone to talk to and talk with. They need no more "practice" than this, although the wider the range of available adults and older children there are for them to engage in this talk, the wider will be their practice.

Should we be optimistic and confident about what first school children can do with their language? We have already seen that by three-and-a-half to four years the basic structures of language are mastered. Also vocabulary, the *content* of their language, is expanding rapidly (Leeper *et al.*, 1979). By kindergarten age, children have an average vocabulary of three thousand words; this expands rapidly to a productive vocabulary of between eight thousand and fourteen thousand words by six years (de Villiers & de Villiers, 1978). This means they are adding an average of five to eight words to the content of their language each day between the ages of one and six years! But it is what language is used to do, what *functions* it serves for the child that is more important than this vocabulary building, since it is this ability to use language across a range of functions that is a key factor in the development of communicative competence.

Wilkinson (1977) quotes a conversation between two four-year-olds. He finds them using language to serve a wide range of functions: to carry on a relationship; to maintain identity; to control or affect the behaviour of others; to give reasons or explain; to find out the reasons, exploring by means of language; to speculate or hypothesize; to enter into the feelings of others; and to give information. I shall say more about language functions later. My point here is to stress the importance of not underestimating the range of uses first schoolers can find for their language. The Russian writer, Chukovsky (1963:10) suggests that "beginning with the age of two, every child becomes for a short period of time a linguistic genius. Later, beginning with the age of five or six, this talent begins to fade". He gives us examples of the imaginative and conceptual prowess of the child in these early years:

"Can't you see? I'm barefoot all over!
I'll get up so early that it will still be late.
Isn't there something to eat in the cupboard?
There's only a small piece of cake, but it's middle-aged."

First schoolers have a wide awareness of the possibilities of their oral language. They can complete a great many sentences spoken to them using only the "contexts" as clues. These contexts are both the words of the sentences already spoken to them, and also their awareness of the other things going on around them. Their developing knowledge of their language provides the necessary thinking support.

In the following transcript Tim, a four-and-a-half year old, is making a very sophisticated use of language. The transcript is valuable since the child is himself preparing a tape which addresses a person who is not present. At first he receives the support of his mother's questions and presence; then he proceeds on his own. He is forced by the context to use his language to reflect explicitly on his past experiences in a manner which reveals the sophisticated use of language that can be available to four-year-olds. The first section of transcript is Tim making this taperecording for his father who is overseas. He realizes his father will "participate" in the conversation (in the role of passive listener) when he hears the tape. So he is talking as if the listener (his father) were in the room with him: Tim is both initiating the conversation and sustaining it:

Tim: Hello Dad. Do you know the Rani cat, the Rani cat,
the Rani cat,
do you know the Rani cat; he lives on Devon Walk.
[Tim's invented song about his Nan's cat]. Hello Dad.
Do you know, oh . . . Dad, I went to the mu . . . oh,

Dad, I went to the museum and I saw a boat wiv a steering wheel, ohh, just a steering wheel wivout a boat and something that we didn't know what it was. It was big and it had a hole in it. We saw a cannon wiv cannon balls it goes wiv it . . . I went wiv Nan because I was at school.

Mum: Who was at school?

Tim: Mum was at school hahaha. I'm going to Ellen's on Fwiday. I'm going to Ellen's on Fwiday. [song] "Five little men in a flying saucer flew round the world one day, they looked left and wight but they didn't like the sight, so one man went away." Mum, I can't do the actions because Dad won't see them. [sings three more verses of this song] . . . "One little man in a flying saucer, flew round the world one day he looked left and wight but he didn't like the sight, so one man went away. None little men in a flying saucer flew round the world one day" . . . what, how do you do that? What goes next?

Mum: They looked left and right.

Tim: "They looked left and wight and then they came back again."

Mum: I'm going to help Nan wash up now, so I'm going to leave Tim to operate the tape recorder all on his own and just have a little chat to you. All right Tim?

Tim: Oh, but Mum I don't know what to say . . . Dad, oh, Dad, Mum bwought *The Wizard of Oz* for me and I went down to see the car being mended when we picked it up, and then, and . . . Dad, I've been playing with Ellen and Sam a lot, and I went up to Wichmond to see Sue. Sue and Eoin still have our colour T.V. . . . that Ellen gave me Dad. Dad, I've just caught a moff . . . over to the McDonalds to see Vicki about the cweam, because we had trifle for tea tonight and the cweam was sour. Dad, at the museum there were stones that glowed and one lot had the light off when they glowed, when they glowed. I hurt my lip and I had a bad fall, when I had a bad fall. I was helping mum wiv the fish and I got down, I tried to get down so that mum could get the plug to wash our hands and then I slipped and fell and that's how I hurt my lip, my nose was bleeding. We made some kiss biscuits last week wiv the shapes. Dad, this is very sad news, we're still having an awful lot of wain! I said this . . . Dad, if you see Nicholas will you say hello fwom me. I fed the ducks at Wichmond and also my teacher's name is Mrs Woberts . . .

I don't know . . . I watch The Flintstones on T.V. Dad, and I enjoy them them very . . . enjoy them very much. Sometimes I

> watch *Playschool*. I watch *Roobarb* after afternoon *Playschool* Here, afternoon *Playschool* is different than morning. [song: first verse of "Puff the Magic Dragon"]. What else Mum? "Togever they would twavel on a boat wiv billowed sail . . . Togever they would twavel on a boat wiv billowed sails, little Jackie Paper perched on Puff's gigantic tail . . . magic tail . . ." I don't know if the tail was mentioned or not. I've been listening to Puff on Dad's wecord — I love you Dad. Goodbye for now.

The second section is Tim interacting with his mother: She is reading him a story which invites him to use the story context and its accompanying pictures to predict the ends of sentences read to him by his mother:

Mum: I hope you enjoyed Tim's ramblings. Nan and I listened as best we could from the kitchen.
Tim: What are ramblings?
Mum: Talking. Tim has just informed me that I can sit over here and enjoy a little chat with you now, but it's really bed-time for Tim and in a moment we're going to choose a book.
Tim: Will you wead it to Dad on the tape and me.
Mum: All right. You go and choose one and we'll leave the tape on and Dad can listen to the story.
Tim: We'll have to say it near the tape.
Mum: All right.
Tim: Dad, the story's called *The Earthworm.*
Mum: Under the grass the earthworm burrowed through the soft brown earth . . . On top of the ground the earthworm left neat curly piles of earth.
Tim: I've never seen an earthworm doing that.
Mum: At night he came out of the ground . . . He followed the hole down and along beneath . . .
Tim: An ant's nest. I'll say it to Dad [louder]: Beneaff an ant's nest.
Mum: Then it went straight along under . . .
Tim: Some carrots, some carrots.
Mum: On and on the earthworm followed the hole below a burrow where . . .
Tim: A rabbit slept.
Mum: He passed a . . .
Tim: drain pipe
Mum: and under a . . .
Tim: House
Mum: As the earthworm travelled under a path he heard . . .
Tim: footsteps above him

Mum: Under a pond it became very . . .
Tim: Muddy
Mum: But ahead the earthworm could see daylight. He had nearly reached the end of the hole. Suddenly against the daylight the shape of something big was creeping towards him. It was . . .
Tim: a mole
Mum: and this was his hole. His nose twitched as he smelt the earthworm. Quickly the earthworm began to burrow but the angry mole bit . . .
Tim: off his tail
Mum: Now he was far away and safe. He had lost the end of his . . .
Tim: tail
Mum: but it would soon grow again. The earthworm's tail grew back and he found a new home where all kinds of . . .
Tim: vegetables were
Mum: When the vegetables had grown fat a fork dug them up before a frost came and spoiled them. The frost froze the earth hard. It was too . . . cold for the earthworm and he burrowed down beneath the . . .
Tim: daffodil bulbs
Mum: Deep, deep down where he was safe from the cold the earthworm curled up and went to sleep until the frost had gone.
Tim: I saw a porpoise Dad. I saw a porpoise Dad and he was hurt because he had one flipper in the air and also I'm, tomorrow I'm staying at Ellen and Sam's over night. Dad, I've got a pair of sunglasses. I'm packing my suitcases for tomorrow night, you know why, don't you? I've got Pirate Smurf with me now. I bought, Mum bwought him at BP and do you know something she said they were too expensive at first, at first, at first. I made a puppet at school. I made a puppet at school Dad, and it, and I named it, and also it's got a sock for, for a body and also . . . um . . . buttons for eyes, buttons for eyes. I've got my shoes under the . . . oh, I've got my new sunglasses la, lalala. I've got my blah blah blah . . . oh, I'm saying it too quickly. I've got my new sunglasses on now. No, I've got my new sunglasses on now. Oh, I keep . . .

In this second section of the transcript Tim is actively involved in listening to a story and contributing by completing the sentences his mother leaves unfinished. Again he is aware of the role the tape will play in involving his father in the situation. This is evident in his early suggestion:

"Will you wead it to Dad on the tape *and* me"; and again when he says, "an ant's nest. *I'll say it to Dad.* Beneaff an ant's nest".

The social context and the relationships that exist between the participants in the conversation play an important role in a child's use of language. In this instance Tim is in a familiar setting (his Nan's house) with familiar people (his mother and his Nan) surrounding him. He is motivated by the fact that the tape is for his father (another familiar person), and the subject matter is important to him because it is about himself and his world. So he is confident and relaxed and uses language with few inhibitions. He is able to control his own environment by operating the taperecorder himself and including or excluding his mother much as he pleases. There are many lessons, even in this artificial situation, for understanding the kinds of environment suited to providing a ready and free flow of young children's language. We also see Tim applying several important *functions* of language.

Halliday (1975:9) sees the learning of the mother tongue as a process of interaction between the child and other human beings. It is part of the child's attempt to come to terms with the surrounding world and to learn about it through categorization and reflection. Language is our most important means of social interaction. Halliday sees the function of language as being of prime importance — the getting the message across — and he sees that structure develops in order to give form to the meaning that the child is expressing:

> ". . . the child learns language as a system of meanings in functional contexts, these contexts becoming, in turn, the principle of organization of the adult semantic system . . ."

Halliday outlines seven functions of language:

1. *Instrumental:* satisfying the children's material needs;
2. *Regulatory:* controlling the behaviour of others;
3. *Interactional:* used by children to interact with those around them;
4. *Personal:* used to express children's own uniqueness; to express their awareness of themselves;
5. *Heuristic:* exploration of the environment, "tell me why";
6. *Imaginative:* creates an environment of their own, "let's pretend";
7. *Informative:* awareness that language can be used as a means of communicating information to someone who does not already possess that information.

Halliday believes that the use of language to inform is a very late stage in the linguistic development of the child, because it is a function which depends on knowing there are functions of language which are solely defined by language itself. All the other functions are outside language. But the informative function has no existence without language itself. Children cannot begin to master it until they have grasped the principle of dialogue, which means grasping the basic nature of the communication process. Other versions of these functions that Halliday proposes are available; Robinson (1978), for example, suggests 14 functions. These lists are of practical value to teachers interested in promoting communicative competence. They are ready to be used as sub-headings in a class syllabus designed to promote children's functional ranges.

Let us return to Tim's transcript. Although there is no real dialogue Tim, at the age of 4 years 4 months, is using the informative function of language and using it well. Another way of describing this function is the "representational" function of language discussed in Chapter 2: where language is used to represent something in the present which is absent. One example of the representational function at work is a radio broadcast; the commonest version is the language of literacy.

Tim applies the informative function when he shows interest in learning a new word by asking, "What are ramblings?". Here he is using language to investigate language and inform himself, which is a meta-language operation: a use of language to understand language.

Tim is usually in control of the situation yet sometimes asks his mother for assistance. He uses language for the purpose of organizing his mother to read a story on the tape; "Will you wead it to Dad on the tape and me?". Here he is using the regulatory function of language. Tim also shows the imaginative function of language at work by inventing the ending of the song, "Puff the Magic Dragon". He uses some of the words that he knows are in the song and adds some of his own in order to finish it. Then he confesses he is unsure by saying: "I don't know if the tail was mentioned or not". At times during the tape Tim uses repetition, sometimes one word, sometimes whole sentences. There seems to be no obvious reason for this. Perhaps he wants to reinforce what he has said, perhaps he varies his intonation a little or perhaps he just repeats it for the pleasure of saying it again. Britton (1970) talks about this type of language use in *Language and Learning*.

Tim is completely involved in the story that his mother reads him, interacting with her by completing the sentence endings, and making a relevant comment. Although he may be taking visual clues from the book, his extended answers demonstrate a highly developed skill in *predicting,* which is a necessary linguistic skill for both oral and written language.

This skill in predicting is a common one among pre-schoolers. They need it to engage in conversations since conversations often use incomplete sentences. Such a skill is developed by a wide and natural use of oral language. It is essential for children to have this facility developed before they begin to read, since prediction is also a skill basic to adequate comprehension in reading. The ability to predict in oral language is fostered by the child engaging widely and diversely in *talk*.

We do have reasons then to be confident and optimistic about what first school children can do with their language. Yet rarely do first schoolers have their knowledge and skills exploited, through ordinary talk, by their teachers and adult carers. The Oxford Preschool Research Project suggests that there is much more potential in first schoolers than is recognized, for the joint exploration of ideas, memories and feelings in talk with adults. The Project's documentary tapes suggest that children have a far greater capacity for elaborate conversation, for remembering, imagining and planning, than they are usually asked to show in the pre-school. They also find that teachers and adult carers are aware of this. Teachers regret their failure to meet the children's needs and capacities in talk (Wood, *et al.*, 1980). The remainder of this chapter is devoted to explaining the ways in which these needs and capacities may be met. The first requirement is to be confident and optimistic about what first schoolers *can do* with their oral language.

The teacher's role in talk

Earning their confidence

The teacher earns the small child's trust and respect by revealing genuine friendliness, unconditional acceptance, warmth, empathy and interest in all dealings with the child. A "quality" developed in the one-to-one relationship makes language flow. It becomes worthwhile and exciting for children to talk freely. In the act of talking freely they learn their language. Here are some suggestions which will help promote the "quality" right from the start.

Firstly, teachers can reveal something of themselves to children. Topics raised with pre-schoolers should build upon the children's own personal experiences and knowledge; yet within this framework teachers can talk extensively about themselves and their thoughts. Teachers might make up stories about their own childhoods, some brief anecdotes which reflect the feelings and thoughts of the less secure child. Children can then identify with these experiences. They are more easily encouraged to relate and speak, even about their most dreaded concerns. Simply taking the pre-schooler's hand in these situations, holding it gently while talking, can work a wonderful change in the child. Secondly, there is the atmosphere of intimacy created by working *together* with small children. It is known that young children tend to develop better where a class programme encourages adult and child to work together from time to time, one-to-one, concerned jointly with activities and language. Thirdly, there is the closeness and empathy derived from adult and child talking together about *shared experiences.*

Experience-based talk

Connie Rosen (in Rosen & Rosen, 1973) reports an experience-based session of talk from a class of six and seven-year-olds. Teacher and children in the class had shared the experience of watching a bird build its nest under the school roof and the chicks hatch day by day. In this instance, the teacher was a participant, learning with the children, and from them as well, since each one's perspective on reality is different. With skill the teacher maintained the theme of the conversation, using careful questions at first, drawing the children's attention to the number of birds in the nest, their appearance, and the mother feeding them. Later she faded herself from the questioning role. She invited children to join in, commenting on the children's talk in much the same way as they comment on hers. She moved onto a new problem: the siting of the nest and its security from enemies and the elements. At times she asked specific children by name to join in, which they did willingly when asked. She had no purpose except the *talk* itself. She was not bent on herding the children towards some specific educational endpoint, except the promotion of talk. The shared experience made this promotion of talk an easy matter. Experiences of this kind need to be promoted by teachers if children are to learn to talk by talking.

Teachers and adult-carers often do not know enough about the past events to which children refer in order to provide a good framework for talk. A consistency and continuity in the relationship is needed to compensate for this. Again, shared experiences over a long period contribute here. These foster the two-way talk which allows the teacher to know the children, a knowledge which is essential to furthering their oral language development.

Listening to the children

Being listened to is a powerful form of motivation for people talking, small children no less than adults. Research confirms that teachers tend to pay surprisingly little heed to pre-school children's efforts at communicating (Wood *et al.*, 1980). Sometimes they are ignored altogether. More often there is an offhanded response to the words, but not to the child's expressed meaning. Teachers jump in with an answer which often heads off the point of the child's message. Small children lose interest in seeking information, in putting forward their plans, ideas and hopes, if no one is listening. By *really listening* the teacher can seek more from the children, help them identify the issues, ideas, feelings, and help give them names. There is considerable hypocrisy in educational efforts to develop listening skills in children if teachers betray none themselves.

Responding to questions

The attentive teacher responds to the "whys" of children with patience, and a care to expanding their interests, not closing them off. As some children will ask more "why" questions than others, these can be used as introductions for wider talk with groups of children (Brearley, 1969). Some children, though, will seem to have no interest in asking "why". It is often the case that these children have been frustrated in earlier situations by not having their "why" questions responded to. They have lost interest in asking "why", but their "interest" remains. There is a real risk of reinforcing in school, and perpetuating for some children, their lack of interest in "why" questions. Perhaps for these children a genuine lack of interest in matters outside themselves and their immediate world will follow in later years. There is research to suggest that those children who initiate a great deal of talk get teacher initiations in return, while those who initiate infrequently are not frequently sought out by teachers (Cazden, 1972).

Management and authoritarianism

Often there is a tendency in teachers to overplay the management side of child-care. Teachers involved in the Oxford Project (Wood, *et al.* 1980), who discussed a recording of their classroom operations, learned to contain their managerial role and take a more active and richer part in conversations with children. Results in the Project suggest that it is more likely to be the managerial, fast-moving nature of many contacts with adults which promotes mundane and context-tied language in small children. Adults need to show that they are available for more than routine management, that they are prepared to talk, play and help. Again, listening to the child is important here. Children arriving in school often have news to share. It *can* be great fun. It can also be frustrating if the teacher is cutting up paper or mixing paint without even a glance in their direction. Often the time *is* unsuitable, and a gentle reminder of this, with the promise of a later opportunity for talk, will keep the child on the boil, as long as these promises are kept soon afterwards.

Teachers may adopt a managerial style because they are good at managing. To spend their time on administration gives them a sense of security and success. Less competent teachers can spend too much time in management activities. They convince themselves that it is the most important part of their work, and the administration *becomes* the curriculum. Goal-displacement occurs. More rare perhaps, but certainly more harmful, are authoritarian managers (Tough, 1977). The authoritarian teacher tends to take centre stage and most, if not all, of the speech time in the child's school day. The authoritarian teacher in early childhood work can have a serious and damaging effect on small children's sensibilities; on their developing self-esteem; and on their feeling for their place in the world. Developing self-esteem and an awareness of one's important place in the world are essential factors in the production of oral language.

Tough (1977, 1979) discusses teachers' assumptions about their roles and their relevance for classroom talk. Her points offer warnings to teachers who hold authoritarian attitudes towards classroom management. Where children must learn first to be obedient and conform without question, without justification being offered, talk in that classroom may be over-concerned with control and children may never experience talk that will extend their thinking. Nor will they understand why certain forms of behaviour are unacceptable. Where children's incidental contributions in language are regarded as distractions, children learn to avoid contributions at any time, and to avoid the teacher if possible as well. Where the aim of achieving conformity to "good manners" encourages the teacher to interrupt spontaneous talk, such talk will dry up. Good manners can be promoted in other ways; in discussion, for example. They are best promoted in school by the teacher's example. Does the authoritarian teacher offer the child an example of good manners?

Teacher talk

A person's voice can invite conversation, or discourage it. A soft, well-modulated voice relaxes and comforts the small child. Only experience of talking with children will teach the teacher the most effective language style to adopt with first schoolers. For the beginning teacher there are obviously two extremes to be avoided: talking in baby talk; and using the language of an encyclopaedia. It is certainly necessary for children to hear a wide variety of "well-formed" utterances to which they can respond. More than this, though, a breadth of functions of language used by the teacher promotes better receptive language in children; "quality" teacher language involves such informative abstract uses as reasoning, predicting, empathizing and imagining. Use of these functions reduces the need for as much imperative and administrative talk.

There are many questions teachers can ask themselves to gauge the effectiveness of their talk with children. Mattick (in Cazden, 1972) gives a detailed list of these. Some important questions not already covered here are: "is our talk a two-way interchange?"; "who does most of the talking?"; "do I avoid using pat phrases, over and over?"; "is my body position in relation to the child an encouraging one, a threatening one, or does it express uninterest?"; and, "are my questions 'thought-promoting' or are they merely 'correct answer' questions?".

Asking questions

In asking questions of small children there is one teacher tendency which can be deadening for child talk. If the adult maintains the dialogue mainly just by asking questions, children's answers tend to be short and uninvolved. Often teachers' questions may over-ride the spontaneous offerings of children. Teachers pay more attention to framing their own questions than to the children's views in return. This takes the pressure off the child. I am not under-rating the role of questioning here, though. Where a teacher's question follows on from a child's opening statement, it will express interest in furthering the talk. It may also expand the topic, especially if it relates to the child's remembered experiences. Rosen also warns against "teacher" questions (to-see-if-you-know-what-I-know), which may create the wrong impression for children of what questions are for.

Research into the nature of "teacher questions" asked of five-year-olds found that they *did* differ from genuine questions. The teacher most often already knew the answer and had no personal need of it. Usually the questions were *convergent* ones, asking for a "yes" or "no" answer. Socratic or open-ended questions on the other hand provoke *divergent* thinking. A sequence of open questions, chosen with care and placed in a logical pattern, can stimulate and develop logical thinking in three-year-olds (Honig, 1982). I say more on the subject of "questioning" in the section "Approaches to Oral Language Development".

Contexts and functions: Children from special backgrounds

The effect of "context" on children's speech style is a complicated issue. Different children come to school with experiences in certain kinds of "talk" situations. They have already established for themselves the ways they prefer to relate verbally or nonverbally to others. The teacher's role is to provide situations in which the children feel "at home" in their talk style. New styles can also be encouraged, including especially those styles of talk expected in school. The first schooler should be edged towards feeling "at home" in these new styles as well, since they are an essential part of overall *communicative competence*. The various kinds of purposeful talk and writing used in schools are called "Curriculum genres" by Christie (1987); she suggests that five-year-olds can display a wider use of genres in their written work if they have taken part in those genres in their interactions with their teachers. The range of the first school "curriculum" itself encourages exploration of the various functions. Deliberate attention to individual *functions of language* may contribute lesson and syllabus aims for music, drama, movement and structured play.

There are many research findings which indicate that children from different social backgrounds differ in their oral language interactions with teachers. Children from low income families, when compared with other children, often ask fewer questions, interact less and tend to approach adults more for purposes of management. On the other hand they may approach teachers less often for contact, conversation or involvement. In their home situations, however, these children are still likely to be involved in extended interactions with their mothers. Tizard & Hughes (1984) see no social class differences, for example, in the amount of mother/child talk, the length of conversations, the frequency and nature of questions and controlling remarks. However, middle class mothers may use language for more complex purposes and employ a wider vocabulary. Wells (1984) found a great similarity between children, regardless of social class or gender, in the amount of language they have learned by the time they reach school age. There are no severe linguistic or social deficiencies for low income first schoolers that need concern the teacher. There can be a difference in style of interaction due to the different context that the school provides. In developing talk in all children teachers need to provide contexts more meaningful for the child; contexts that provide novel opportunities for using and developing verbal skills.

Cultural differences in the way children can use their language are more important than socio-economic differences (Honig, 1982). Children from different cultural backgrounds may be very limited in the range of functions to which they can put their language. At the same time, Cazden reports from Clay's New Zealand studies that teachers themselves interact less often with culturally different first school children (Clay, 1985;

Cazden, 1987). The teacher's role in oral language work becomes a vital one for these children if they are to gain influence over their own lives and affairs as members of a new culture.

At present, designers of programmes for the language development of children from poverty backgrounds cannot suggest methods or models that have produced long-term gains. Implications for classroom practice can be drawn from some of the work, however. McGinness (in Feagans & Farran, 1982) draws together implications from studies of intervention programmes and provides suggestions under five headings: staffing; programme content; environment; evaluation; and child and family. The strongest and most regular finding is that positive and frequent verbal interaction with an adult, around a joint activity of cognitive significance, is a factor in all programmes that have produced lasting gains in disadvantaged children.

In summary, this section urges first school teachers to see as their role in fostering talk:

1. to listen to children;
2. to give them something real to talk about;
3. to encourage and make time for conversation and dialogue;
4. to use questions with care, in generating and developing language;
5. to develop an atmosphere of trust and respect; and
6. to maintain a consistency and continuity in their relationships with children.

Approaches to oral language development

In this section I discuss three approaches to oral language work: 1) artificial methods; 2) conceptual and syntactic development; and 3) experience-based oral language development. I recommend an easy blend of the second and third approaches.

Artificial methods

An aim of first school oral language work is to create situations where *effective dialogue* can take place. "Dialogue" has one special feature which makes artificial methods of language instruction inconsistent with it. Dialogue is spontaneous. Talk which is not spontaneous is not dialogue. When two people engage in dialogue they are adjusting their responses and their meanings continually. They are doing this to suit the responses they hear in reply, and the ever-changing context of the dialogue.

A strictly formal approach, using artificial methods of language instruction such as drills, rehearsed speeches, rote learning of questions and answers, catechisms, etc., has little in common with effective talk: with dialogue. It is condemned as a method for this and other reasons (Cazden, 1972). This kind of approach demands language "corrections" of one kind or another. With small children these "corrections" of grammar, pronunciation, accent, word use, will be many. Such a weight of corrections will risk damaging children's motivation, interest and self-esteem. It also ignores the established oral language *starting point* for teachers: valuing the language that children bring to school.

In our knowledge of language we are far enough advanced to appreciate that there is some important connection between an individual's language use and psychological factors such as identity and self-esteem. We appreciate that it is often a dangerous and unethical matter for the teacher to play the "language censor" and try to tamper with such things as accent and pronunciation in children. The presence or absence of an accent or pronunciation trait is not very relevant to the semantic grasp of a word. It is possible that children drilled in pronunciation exercises will have little matching comprehension of words, while those who pronounce strangely or with difficulty are managing greater semantic effect by their rigour in choosing a word at all whose pronunciation is known only imprecisely.

Young children are great imitators. They are able to parrot language with astonishing success, but often with little matching comprehension. Artificially introduced verbal exercises of one kind or another may lead at best to a thin and superficial result, because the language is not properly grasped and not *functional:* it serves no more purpose than satisfying the artificial demands imposed by others. This approach may produce what Vygotsky calls "empty verbalism". It may be argued that test results in formally structured programmes look deceptively good. Usually, though, the test situations replicate the learning situation for children, offering them only another opportunity to reproduce their empty verbalism. By repeating fixed patterns children are using language in a limited set of contexts. There is little to suggest that they can generalize the patterns learned in other types of contexts.

Approaches which rely heavily or exclusively on convergent, fixed-response questioning channel rather than open children's thinking. Where open-ended questions are used, children make original utterances and think originally. They are producing an idea and not repeating a set pattern. Language becomes an instrument of more mature thinking only when it is freed from concrete situations, from second-hand patterns and from highly contrived events. It then becomes a shaper and director of thought. There may be some place in the first school for less rigid artificial methods, where drills are not a feature. The programme instituted in London by the Gahagans (1971), if used very selectively, might provide a few ideas with application in the first school, especially a use of communication games like "Reporter" or "Walkie Talkie". Artificial approaches, though, try to equip children with a form of language that is both alien to them *and* below their potential. Dannequin (1987) speaks of six-year-olds in mother tongue classes as "gagged children".

Conceptual and syntactic development

I have already mentioned that children have gained a remarkable proficiency in structuring their language, even by the age of three. What remains for the first school to provide in the area of syntax is plenty of opportunities for children to apply the knowledge of structure that they already possess. This means plenty of talk, since by talking they learn to talk. Sentences come into being and grow in complexity as the context for talk itself expands. The same structures of syntax are used in different ways, edging the child's utterances towards a more complex expression of meaning.

The content of this language is another matter. There are approaches which can be adopted to expand content, but always again based in talk, not in the deliberate teaching of "words". *Experience-based* talk is the requirement. Key concepts of time, space, number, causality, and the various ways we have for classifying things, can be laid for children in the first school. Tough (1977) suggests ways in which the teacher can contribute to this conceptual development. Where children's reports of events are lacking in detail, she suggests this may not be due to a lack of words, but more to a lack of awareness of detail. She recommends using questions which can direct attention to detail: "what did it look like?" or "what did you like about it?". Where children do not seem to know the language of comparison (e.g. "same'; "different"; "alike"; "nearly"; "about"; "as"; "almost") other questions can be asked: "what's different about them?", "how are they the same?" and "why do you like this one better?". Tizard & Hughes (1984) caution against an excessive use of question and answer sessions of this type, however. As a safeguard they offer two conditions that should be met: firstly the child must be interested in answering the question; secondly the adult using the questions should have the skill and time to follow up any inadequacies revealed in the child's understanding.

Where children have difficulty in stating and understanding spatial relationships (e.g. "behind"; "in front of"; "beside"; "beneath"; "below"; "over"; "under"; "through"), Tough recommends using incidents in the child's play to check and then feed in information by manipulating objects and showing meaning. Where children have the labels for objects, in a class, but not their class name (e.g. "cat"; "dog"; "horse"; "whale" but not "animal"; or "boys"; "girls"; "adults" but not "people") the teacher can use the class name itself in such questions as "what other *animals* can you tell me about?". Sometimes the classes are known and children need help in differentiating class objects. They may use the word "flower" to refer to all "plants" for example. Again information can be fed in to aid this differentiation: "yes, the flower is a plant and that tree is a plant too".

Braun's article (1977), aimed at helping experience-based language development, has many sound ideas for the teacher. Two of these are the techniques of "brainstorming" and the presentation of "exemplars" and "non-exemplars" of a concept. *Brainstorming* activities are valuable in illustrating the more abstract concepts; words associated with "time", for example. Children can name, while the teacher lists, all the things they can think of which are "slow": donkey, elephant, grandma, etc. These words can be used to develop simile constructions: "as slow as a donkey", etc. *Exemplars and non-exemplars* of a concept help the child decide between "what is" and "what is not" a specific attribute of a given concept. For example, the concept "triangle" can be introduced by presenting all the various types of triangles, their shapes and sizes, as *exemplars* of the concept. From this the child will abstract the relevant attributes of triangles. It is sound teaching practice to present some *non-exemplars* as well, some non-triangular shapes, so that the child is drawn to see the difference. The attributes of "triangle" are highlighted in seeing the distinction.

There is no substitute for widespread exposure through experience to the meaning of words. I mean here both those many meanings that refer to concrete things in the environment and those many others that are more abstract. However, to attempt to "force-feed" words to children is not "meaning construction". The task is really to enlarge the stock of *distinctions* available to children. These distinctions in formal education, are best provided after careful planning by teachers of learning experiences in which the distinctions are presented to children. At the same time, or later, they can be linked in talk to the words which name the distinction in the child's mind. The word gradually takes on the character of the original "distinction" itself if the child is able to use it in the right context in a motivated way.

The important step for children comes when they progress from merely "having" the word to "knowing how to use it". In the first school the relative absence of the practical skill of writing means that progress from "having" a word to "knowing how to use" it depends upon *talk*. It is easy to see then how harmful the imposition of over-strict "no-talking rules" in first schools can be to the child's conceptual development.

Experience-based oral language development

Most dialogue between young first schoolers is concerned with the here-and-now. It centres on the child, the adult, other children, the group, objects and events currently taking place. When talking about remembered events, not surprisingly, "home is where the memory is". It is vital, then, to provide a focus in the present or in the near past for language development activities. For novel and original dialogue to flow, children need to be experiencing or to have just experienced something to talk about which for them is novel and original. Sometimes beginning teachers want to begin at the other end. They set up group talk situations where the children are asked to discuss planting seeds, or thinking about what will float or sink, before they have been exposed to the experiences themselves. The greatest gains in first schoolers' language come when children are asked to use words to express ideas about what is happening, what has happened or what will happen. Talking about "what will happen" depends on them seeing what is happening.

With very young first schoolers the value of one-to-one contact with the teacher is important. Teachers can seize many little interludes for conversation on the here-and-now. Opportunities for chatting occur when they are helping children use the toilet; while they are putting on their shoes; and when teachers greet them as they arrive in school. Mealtimes in first school are a good opportunity for dialogue. It is wise, in this regard, to keep lunch and snack groups as small as possible, to avoid putting two adults, who may dominate dialogue, at one table; to have good conversation starters ready in advance; and tactfully to ensure that no-one is ignored or consistently drowned out. At the same time mealtimes should be social and fun occasions. Verbal fluency can be squashed if vocabulary building or mechanical drill over-rides the occasion's delight for the child. In all these situations, the commonplace experiences become memorable and worthy of interest because of the accompanying talk.

The experiences that can be provided for all first schoolers are limited only by the teacher's imagination. In practice providing "dimensions of experience" is consistent with accepted psychological and educational theory. This involves a movement *from* the experience *to* the concept. First there is the experience: for example, during an excursion the children witness what happens in a savings bank. This real experience is followed by three dimensional representations (models, dolls, toys) and two dimensional representations (pictures, puzzles, books) and then by the words associated with the experience (passbooks, deposits, withdrawals). In this way a more complete mental image of the word meanings is built up. The child understands or sees meaning in the event which was the experience. Throughout this process talk is proceeding. The child moves from having the words to knowing how to use them.

Again Tough's book (1977) presents conventional approaches to experience-based dialogue which "work" with first schoolers. Braun's article (1977) discusses activities for moving children's thinking and language from the concrete experience, through the pictorial, to the symbolic-verbal (3D>2D>1D). With five to seven year olds, talk about "imagined experiences" is important for bringing their thinking and their language into a more expressive and poetic mode. Teachers can invent devices for summoning up "imagined experiences". They can use a cardboard cylinder, for example, as a "magic telescope" through which they can describe experiences, encouraging children to take turns in looking and talking about what they "see". They can present children with a "mystery box", sealed and inviting, whose contents can only be "guessed at". They can use a crystal glass or a prism as a magic ball for children to peer into and "see" the future or the past.

Classroom organization

Providing opportunities for effective talk should be a central concern in thinking about classroom management in the first school. Teachers often claim that it is the conditions under which they teach which can prevent effective talk in the classroom. There is good reason for complaint here. Class size is the chief constraint on a teacher in oral language work, but even for unacceptably large first school classes there are recommendations which can be made to promote effective talk.

How many children can reasonably work together in effective talk activities? I have already mentioned the value for young first schoolers of one-to-one talk, with the teacher seizing routine management moments in the day to engage in dialogue. At the other extreme there is whole class talk. This demands a skilled teacher. The emotional risks for children are many, especially where a genuine climate of trust and respect has not yet developed. For a small child, addressing an unknown adult across the silence of perhaps 35 other children, is an act that only the most confident will attempt. When the teacher is also looking for "right answers", the fear of rejection of what he or she has to offer will keep the sensitive first schooler silent. This is not an environment for effective talk, by any standard.

Group work is a good basis for dialogue. I mention in Chapter 2 that in many cultures the principal source of language learning is other children. Where talk between children is stifled, this source dries up. Recent research, with language-delayed preschoolers, has found that small group work improved oral language performance; and that children learned more when group sizes were kept to three or four rather than ten children. Other research, with seven-year-olds, has found that children in groups of two or three were distracted from their task much less than groups of six or seven (Reed, 1976). The Oxford Project commends a use of pair-work for younger first schoolers. The "rare privacy" of a pair of children playing undistracted at a pretend game produces rich and connected conversation.

A "learning centres" strategy or *integrated day* capitalizes on small group work: two to four children in each group change their activities and use different skills as the day progresses. *Vertical grouping*, or mixed age ranges within groups, is a sound technique. The younger children benefit in oral language development. The older children learn to apply new language functions: a chance to teach, inform and vary their language to suit the capacities of the younger ones. Teachers using vertical grouping find that more time is available for them to participate in group and one-to-one talk. Combining these two approaches requires much pre-planning and systematic review. Where open-plan work and team-teaching are incorporated as well, this pre-planning and review become co-operative. The organizational demands are greater, but the positive results can also be great as well.

There is a need for a certain stability and harmony in classroom management if oral language is to be fostered; interruptions and unplanned intrusions can be destructive of achievement, while irrelevant noise levels, poor lighting and uncomfortable surroundings act strongly against effective talk. Qualitative differences in children's communicative competence will result as levels of stability and harmony in the classroom environment change.

Keeping detailed records of children's language progress is recommended as part of these approaches (see next section). Tough stresses record keeping as a necessary accompaniment to all first school work. She provides an example of a talk "fostering record" (1977). Checklisting of skills mastery is necessary for achieving integrity in any oral language curriculum.

An environment rich in sound and sense is needed for experience-based language development. A constantly changing environment including "touch tables", "smell tables", "visual stimulus tables", "tables containing knick-knacks and coins", will encourage dialogue, with children discussing, questioning and expounding (Roberts, 1972). These tables, and other talk areas, provide congregating places. After a while talk becomes very natural and spontaneous in such places, as they are associated in children's minds with spontaneity and interest. Teachers can increase the effectiveness of their own talk by arranging storage space so that children can independently have access to materials, including additional individual activities when group tasks reach their climax and while other groups are still working. These techniques serve to lessen the need for management by teachers and free them for talk. While arranging displays of work and stimulus material teachers can find opportunities for very effective talk if children are helping with the arrangements.

There are important, managerial considerations which influence children's language development in organizations like schools and nurseries. Often when there are two staff members on duty they talk to each other about experiences and ignore the children. Where staff hierarchies exist, often only the staff member in charge interacts with the children. Honig (1982) suggests that young children in group care need to reap the benefit of having at least two highly articulate adults engaged actively in rich language encounters to promote language learning.

Adults working with first schoolers have different personal strengths. Where two or more work together an occasional division of labour can draw on these strengths. Some adults can assume the roles of manager, conversationalist or player, and rotate these roles where useful. By encouraging a few children at a time to be present in management activities, dialogue is fostered. Trained classroom assistants can be encouraged to participate in this valuable form of education. Clearly there is a role for student teachers in this, as well as for parent-help in the formal classroom. Provided that a climate of trust and respect can still be maintained and enhanced with helpers in the classroom the oral language opportunities for children will be broadened.

Evaluation of oral language in the first school

If talk is genuinely experience-based, if it is constant and diverse, then teachers can judge their whole class programme to be successful on these criteria alone. The aim is to foster talk, and under these conditions talk is being fostered. Individual children, however, will inevitably need special assessment, and it will be necessary for records to be kept even on the most obviously competent. Cazden (1972) provides a brief and useful overview of assessment methods for individual children. Tape-recording a child's speech at various times in the school year, and having outsiders judge the progressive intelligibility of the tape, is one recommended method. Any complete assessment approach, though, should include observations of children in situations natural to their own culture. They may otherwise be reluctant to play the tester's game and results might not properly reflect their level of language ability.

Anastasiow (1979) recommends three specific techniques for assessment: firstly, the "dictated story" technique is simple and effective. After drawing or painting a picture, children are encouraged to tell stories about it. These are written down for them by an adult and used later for assessment. Secondly, puppets can be used with children who are reluctant to speak to an adult at length. They will speak more readily to a hand puppet. Thirdly, the "sentence repetition" technique provides a more structured approach to assessment of very young children. Anastasiow lists four different sets of sentences which children can be asked to repeat, revealing by their omission of key words and structures certain weaknesses in language. The task is really to keep a record of children's proficiency across a range of contexts, functions and styles.

Across the first school curriculum

In the early stages of the first school, talk and play are the main substance of the curriculum. They provide all that is necessary for the linguistic, social and cognitive development of the human child at this age. The special needs of our civilization add a third more artificial and less universal element: exposure to books. These three — talk, play and books — provide both the pedagogies and the objectives for the wider "upper" first school curriculum. At this stage of schooling the endpoints of education and the processes through which the endpoints are reached are one and the same: the "learning" of effective talk, effective play, and the effective use of books is only achieved by engaging in talk, play and the use of books. Nowhere else in education is the teacher's role a more all-embracing and important one: in their school experience children in the first school do nothing which is not heavily affected by their teacher's influence, attention or inattention.

In the discussion below I divide the first school "curriculum" into five areas and briefly discuss the place of oral language in each: 1) reading, writing and listening skills; 2) investigations; 3) representations; 4) storytime; and 5) play. Three of the five areas identified conform, in a logical way, with philosophical discussion on the distinct "forms" which knowledge might take within the total school curriculum, a point that is expanded on page 79 of Chapter 4. Neither the first nor the last "area" conforms; each of these represents a "skill mastery" area whose development is prior to or continuous with the acquisition of knowledge in the other three areas.

Reading, writing and listening skills

Discussion in Chapter 2, "The Case for Oral Language in Schooling", makes the connection between oral competence and literacy a plain one. I show there that high level development in literacy can depend on an earlier or concurrent high level development in oral language. The first school can lay the foundation for both, through the teaching approaches and teacher roles for promoting effective talk, which are already presented in this chapter. Books and first schools are inseparable. Plenty of "reading matter", long before reading begins, which feeds children's interests, which stretches their powers of making sense of things, and which relates to the world they live in, provides them with much of the material for their talk.

We may introduce again here the distinction between talk to other people and what is called "egocentric" talk, or talk to self. This second kind of talk, in Vygotsky's view (1962), is talk on its way to becoming thought. By talking to themselves, young children gradually come to be able to "think" in talk. The egocentric talk eventually becomes silent and internal.

When they look at the pictures in books and talk about them to themselves, children are on the way to internalizing their language. During this process, they are unable to grasp the idea of "thinking" in language very easily: a four year old may say to his father "but you're not reading the paper, Dad, you're just looking at it!" Books of interest, to provide conversation pieces for themselves and for others, assist this process and promote their understanding of the "point" of books.

A more complete discussion of the acquisition of the sub-skills required in reading and writing is presented by Tough (1977). It is important for children to recognize that signs can be used for words, which themselves are used for objects, actions, people and events. This understanding comes through talk about signs and symbols around them. Children's oral work in telling their own stories brings them to understand the "concept of reading". The use of sequencing cards and other materials assists in this process.

The often confusing idea of "reading readiness" is discussed in a book with that title (Downing & Thackray, 1975). An issue of importance that that book considers addresses a common misunderstanding: the wrong belief that children's oral language at the first school level is inadequate for the task of reading books presented to them. This imbalance can certainly arise later in education. However, at this stage the oral language children use is far more advanced than the language of the books with which they are taught to read. This fact is clearly of value in approaches to introducing writing into the first school, approaches well covered by Britton (1970).

Listening carefully and discriminating between sounds are both basic skills for effective talk and depend on effective talk for their development. Leeper *et al.* (1979) provide a useful discussion, listing eight detailed suggestions for teaching how to listen and how to use the results of listening in first schools. Hendrick (1975) provides an appendix of activities to develop auditory discrimination, approaches used and developed in practice by first school teachers-in-training. Listening skills are best encouraged, though, by the *teacher's model*.

Investigations

Most aspects of the physical and social sciences, and of mathematics, can be considered "investigations" in the first school. As elsewhere the methodologies used are play and talk. Rosen & Rosen (1973) distinguish two extremes of talking-about-the-past and talking-while-doing, with talking-while-observing in the middle. "Investigations" is concerned with "doing" and "observing". Talk in this area has immediacy. It is stimulated by anything in the real world that attracts and holds the interests of first schoolers, as a class, or preferably in small talking groups. Specific syllabus items are limited only by the teacher's imagination and by their effect on children's talk.

To offer a structure consistent with accepted curriculum theory, "investigations" can follow the following pattern of development, bringing the child in sequence to think and talk about: (i) myself; (ii) my family and home; (iii) my neighbourhood; (iv) my community. In later primary years, as the ideas of the social sciences and the physical sciences become more separate in children's minds, the social sciences may go on to consider (v) my region (county/state); (vi) my country; (vii) my world region and (viii) my world. Different concepts can be introduced and re-introduced at different levels — words associated with "individuals", "institutions" and "groups". Items (i) to (iv) above can provide all the structure necessary for a first school "investigations curriculum".

The role of experience-based talk in all of this is a central one. Braun's article provides specific approaches for getting the most out of investigatory experiences. Tough (1977) and Garvie (1984) discuss the practical use of talk for bringing children to the beginnings of investigatory thinking, for adding the skills, for seeing relationships, for predicting, for understanding processes and recognizing principles. For reaching specific goals in Maths, drama is the activity where it all comes together: role-players and audiences of first schoolers are keenly involved in the acting out of related situations, such as a shop keeper giving change to a customer, a farmer counting his produce, or a builder making measurements.

Representations

Art, music, drama and even movement can so obviously be made richer as oral language activities. Getting children to talk about their art work is a favoured use of oral language in concrete representation work. Through dialogue we can offer young children skills that they will use to derive extended meaning from their efforts to represent their thinking concretely. Such dialogue arises very easily. It can centre upon children's enjoyment of the event depicted in their model, painting or drawing; their involvement; the characters; and even how the picture or model connects with their feelings. In music, too, this kind of talk about the task in hand can be enriching; a point to be remembered is that the lyrics of songs are poems before they become lyrics. They can be enjoyed in oral work by children in that form as well.

In the first school many opportunities exist for role play. Unless children have an opportunity to act a certain role they may not be able to learn to use the appropriate language styles and functions that that role involves. Their ability to use language will be enhanced by the range of roles that they learn. The "home corner" (or the "wendy house") is an inviting area for young children to lose themselves in roles. More formal drama work should be of short duration; there is a need to be sensitive to the fear that some young children have about real or imagined public ridicule. Yet even the youngest will react positively if there is group involvement and the subject matter is related to the child's self, family, community or world. Stories to be acted out are best invented by the teacher, with the children's interests and capacities in mind. As children's confidence develops they can come to enjoy their singular contributions which collectively tell a whole story.

Storytime

Here the "foundations" for so much else are laid: a love of literature and books; elements of moral education; logical sequencing, which is a basis of philosophy; and an introduction to religious and spiritual experience. Management pressures in classrooms can easily intrude on storytime. The teacher who allows these pressures to intrude can rob children of the "foundations" listed above and much else as well. Read to the children singly on your lap, in groups at your feet or to the whole class, but above all *read to the children* (see Cazden, 1972).

Storytelling is a valuable technique in oral language work. When teachers tell stories dramatically they can judge their success by how much active involvement and repetition they can spontaneously induce in the children. They can watch for the child imitating their own mime and movement, and encourage them singly or as a group to dramatize all or part of a story or poem simultaneously. In 3D they can present the story through models, objects, dolls or puppets. In 2D, besides a simple use of books, other techniques are available: flannelgraphs, relief or collage pictures, moveable cut-outs, sand-tray scenes, magnetic boards, shadow-shows and drawing the story while it is told. Perspective and time changes can be illustrated for children in these approaches. Stories selected that invite repetition by the children are very suitable (i.e. repetitive sentences or chants at different stages). Where there is question and answer dialogue in a story a breakthrough to language fluency is achieved when on second and later hearings children take over and tell most of the story themselves. Specific concepts and skills in language can be woven into the teacher's invented story.

For older first schoolers there can be many advantages when the children themselves invent and tell their own stories. I discuss this skill area, so important in everyday communication, in the next chapter.

Play

We can now be confident that fantasy play provides much more than the opportunity for expressing inner fantasies. It is also a rich medium for promoting language development among children. Children's ability to use language for such functions as self-maintaining and imagining can be increased through fantasy play and pretend games (Vygotsky, 1962). Often they "lose themselves" when the fantasy situation becomes a vehicle for talking and self-consciousness falls away, especially when the child believes another being (a doll or puppet) is doing the talking. While they are at play, children's conversations seem to be fostered more by some *play materials* than by others (Leeper *et al.*, 1979): play with dolls, blocks, crayons and clay is accompanied by talk for a high percentage of the time; painting, using scissors and looking at books results in less talk. Also the *type of activity* is influential: house-keeping and group discussion hold the greatest potential for developed language use; block play, woodworking and dancing have the least.

The teacher's role in play *is* important. When teachers play alongside children their reassuring presence encourages opportunities for talk about the play. In parallel play of this kind they can inject new ideas and language. As co-players, in the same game, authoritarian roles vanish. Trust, respect and an appreciation by children for their teachers' feelings can grow as a result, laying a firm basis for an effective talk environment. Sometimes the play theme can be used to make reference to the real world and to ideas that move child thinking into the abstract.

The role of play in learning and its influence on oral language receives a broad theoretical coverage by Anastasiow (1979). Tough (1977) distinguishes three types of play: physical, exploratory and imaginative. She suggests in her transcripts how teacher-child dialogue is made possible in each mode.

Summary

There are good reasons from our knowledge of language acquisition and development to be confident and optimistic about what first schoolers can do with their oral language. Too often children's linguistic knowledge and skills are not well exploited in the first school. As well as learning by talking, the young child learns to talk by talking. In first schools an atmosphere of trust and respect, and one where there is a continuity and consistency in relationships, is conducive to fostering effective talk.

The use of strictly artificial approaches for developing oral language is not recommended. Experience-based language work that centres on conceptual development is the recommended approach for developing communicative competence across a range of contexts.

Providing opportunities for effective talk should be a central concern in thinking about classroom management in the first school. Talk, play and books provide both the objectives and the pedagogies of the first school "curriculum". Without effective talk the first school is without its chief method for learning and its chief objective.

4 Oral language in the middle school

By the senior school years it is often too late for education to contend with what may be long-established problems for individual children in using oral language. If confidence, motivation or skill in using speech is lacking, it is possible that for many this will remain an enduring handicap throughout life. It is probable that the limits of future language potential are established for the child, in a near final fashion, by the onset of puberty. The role of the middle years of schooling, then, is the vital one for promoting oral language development in children.

The middle years of schooling span the age range of eight to thirteen years. Middle Schools for children within this age range are rapidly being established in some parts of the world as alternative systems of educational provision. The arguments for this approach to school organization are compelling ones. However, in writing this chapter to focus on "middle schools" I am not indicating any strong commitment to middle schools as a uniquely good system of organization. The age range covered in this chapter is selected as a unity because I see this middle school period as a distinct language development stage. This itself is a strong case for middle schools in any case. Since language and intellectual functioning are so closely connected and interdependent, there is good reason to treat as a developmentally unified educational period an age range of language development which itself reveals the features of a unity.

Language and intellectual development in the middle years

We can say that by seven years the structure of a child's language is all but fully developed (Glazer & Morrow, 1978). Since language development no longer depends as much on structural development in the middle years, the chief factor in semantic development is the acquisition of vocabulary: words, whose meanings are concepts. However, *true* concept formation seems beyond the capacities of most pre-adolescents. Before puberty it is likely that word meanings are far more volatile than they are afterwards. The end of syntactic development and the real beginnings of concept formation, as a result, mark the beginning and end points of the middle period of language development.

During this middle period children begin to think about language as language. They begin to be more selective in choosing words for use, thinking more about their meanings. They can give definitions for words, they can recognize subtle differences between them. Unfamiliar words are commented upon and explanations are demanded for their use. The sounds of words hold a special fascination and this is reflected in middle schoolers' delight in rhymes and chants. At the same time, towards the end of the period, children may be using many technical terms drawn from a wide range of knowledge areas. Often these terms will be used appropriately, but the inter-relationships and the boundaries of the concepts they name will rarely be clear enough to support sustained formal thinking in the specialist areas.

Here is an example from Tim, a nine year old: Tim was asked if they play cricket at his school; he replied: "We do play cricket at school, but it's not *commercial*". Now this is not as simple a slip as it seems. Tim is not just mistaking the word "commercial" for the word "competitive". What he is missing are the two quite different and complex fields of thought that these two words "lodge" in. His knowledge of cricket, played competitively, comes mainly from watching it played professionally on television, and it is on commercial television at that. As a result he has the notions of "competitiveness" and "commercialness" a bit blurred and he may continue to have difficulty with holding these two categories apart in his mind until he is at least into his early teens.

Research done by Piaget and his associates (Piaget, 1978; Piaget & Inhelder, 1958; Barnes & Todd, 1977) suggests that the thinking of thirteen-year-olds will be mainly at the intuitive level of concrete operations, only rising occasionally above this level, under especially suitable conditions, to what is known as hypothetico-deductive modes of thinking. Oral language work, in which children internalize the products of their talk and allow it to influence their thinking and their future talk, is a vital factor in promoting this move into more complex modes of thought. Where there are severe literacy weaknesses for individual children, oral language work may be the *only* factor.

The boy talking in the transcript below is Darryl, an Australian twelve-year-old working-class boy of average reasoning ability for his age. The questions put to him orally are part of a battery of questions designed to elicit language used in at least two different ways: to describe and to explain.

1. *Would you tell me a bit about the teachers in that last school of yours?*
   Well, when I was in primary school we had these good teachers that . . . that would teach you a lot about history, what, what went on in the past, and if you were really good they'd give you an early mark or they'd give you P.E. if it was in the middle of the day . . . The day, teach you all the, all the sorts of things and you get a merit card if you . . . work well and help the teachers after any events are going in the school. I got, in, when I was in Kinder I got two; first class I got one and I didn't get any second or third; in fourth class I got three and in sixth class I got two; I didn't get any in fifth class. And . . . when I was in sixth class had this good teacher who took us on excursions . . . And like, at Warragamba Dam we went under the, under the dam in the wall and it was cold 'cause I only had a T-shirt on and we went outside. We, we went across a suspension bridge and the teacher that took us, my sixth class teacher, well she was afraid of heights and we all rocked it and she started running and then we took the pictures of the dam and, on the other side of the dam, well it was all, all dirty water, had all . . . sticks and soccer ball in it. And we went up to the National Park at Gosford and went up, we saw all the people up there. We saw kangaroos, all animals and we were allowed to pat them and feed them. We went up to the headquarters where *Skippy* was . . . filmed and on our way back we stopped to get something to eat and we, I, six of us in my class went up to, to Point Wollstonecraft at Newcastle for a ten day camp and had these different sorts of teachers. We had activities like Putt-Putt, Soccer, swimming, canoeing, archery and a few things . . . orienteering and . . .

2. *Would you say it was a good school? Why?*
   Yeah, yes because all the teachers, they were really nice to you and they built a new canteen and sports store and wet weather shed just for the kids and that's about it.

3. *What sort of person would you describe as a good person?*
   . . . Someone who's faithful and who helps people that are in danger like, of a dog that's going to bite you or something.

Someone who, when you're new to the school or something, they show you around and that makes them really good to you, really good person.

4. *Would you say that telling a lie is always wrong?*
   Yes. Because if you tell the wrong thing and . . . you tell the wrong thing to your parents or something they find out and then you get in trouble, you get a belting and, and you wouldn't like that and I don't lie because if I do I get the strap and these other people lie, they lie to friends, they lie to their parents and they're on the dole you know. That's why we don't talk to them.

5. *What about killing; would you say that killing another person is always wrong?*
   Yes. 'Cause if you kill someone, that's committing suicide and you commit suicide you go into jail or into a home for life and you got, you could, you could get shot yourself by, if you rob a bank, you shoot someone and the guard . . . hides and then when you go, he shoots you and . . . Like in an accident, that's bad because if you go over a cliff, there's another person in the car with you or a baby you kill them and not just yourself.

This transcript offers some good indications about what a senior middle school child can do with language. Fluency is the most notable surface-level feature of this transcript; Darryl is at home with the subject matter and the context of the exercise; his language flows and it keeps up with his apparent intellectual level. His descriptive language is filled with detail; there are strong statements of likes and dislikes. His views are quite dogmatically stated; they are not much qualified by language. It could be that more group discussion work in Darryl's school background would have encouraged him to see more than the one point of view he expresses so often at present. He is also a great user of lists: "soccer, swimming, canoeing, archery . . ." or "I didn't get any in second or third, in fourth class I got three and in sixth class I got two". These lend support to his claims about things that are important to him. In fact, these lists are an important subject matter for all his language: things that touch upon himself and record his interests. There is little recourse to structuring his arguments beyond his cataloguing of the evidence. Where a logically structured argument is attempted, (as in 4) it quickly breaks down or spills over into irrelevancies. I have to say, though, that if pressed on the point Darryl could probably explain why they are not irrelevancies; but he does not yet think about doing it as a matter of course; he does not yet take his listener's point of view into consideration by making his statements stand alone, by making them explicit. We can see that Darryl's communicative competence does not yet equip him routinely to take into account in his talk all the relevant factors in the talk context.

The talk Darryl offers in response to 1 is more concerned with "what we did" rather than with the topic suggested by the question (i.e. the characteristics of his teachers). This is something to keep in mind with upper primary level children: they will sometimes seize an appealing but rather irrelevant single idea in an assignment or question topic and respond to that rather than to the whole; they are prone to go off at a tangent. It is not always enough to give children at this age just explicit instructions; sometimes it is necessary to give them instructions about the instructions as well, and have them signal to you in language that they have understood the purpose of the exercise.

Children at this age are very thorough in their reporting back on the progress of events; class and group discussions can use "reports" on activities that the children have engaged in as their regular subject matter; children will enjoy the telling and the listening: any statement beginning with the word "we" will grab the interest of twelve-year-olds since they are extremely communal and curious about their fellows.

There are strong clues to twelve-year-old *conceptual* development in Darryl's transcript. In 1, he defines the difficult term "history" for his listener and for himself, suggesting in this that he knows that some concepts, like "history", are difficult ones for people to exchange messages about. This ability to think about and become consciously aware of the meanings of words and to employ this awareness in certain tasks comes in middle to later childhood (Menyuk, 1977). In 3, and elsewhere, Darryl uses an explanatory sentence where an older child or adult might have recourse to one or two abstract words. In 5, the difficult concept "committing suicide" is used wrongly; Darryl seems to confuse "suicide" with "homicide". This special term for "murder" is plainly available to him as a concept but he is unable to map the concept onto a precise entry in his store of words and he locates an unsuitable word instead.

How does an older middle school child differ from a younger one in intellectual interests? Eight-year-olds delight in the physical environment and in exploring their world. They are enthusiastic about animals and their care; they enjoy practical work and talking about what they have done and seen. What eight-year-olds often cannot do readily is see the world from different perspectives and understand the viewpoints of others. This is not to say that they are unsympathetic to the feelings of others (especially where pets are concerned), but they will tend to see those feelings as *their own* feelings translated into other people. As a result, discussion group work needs to be of a different type for young middle schoolers. It is concerned more with talking while doing, rather than talking alone. Dialogue at this level needs to centre on manipulable apparatus and data; talking about how and why things work and about the relations between symbols, figures and the real world. Here is a list of things that eight-year-olds can comfortably do with their language (after Halliday, 1973, 1977). They can use language:

1. to satisfy their material needs;
2. to control the behaviour of others (and to have their behaviour controlled);
3. to get along with others;
4. to give expression to the self;
5. to learn about and explore the natural world;
6. to pretend;
7. to tell others what they know.

By the time they reach eleven years children know a great deal about using language for collaborative thinking, for encouraging one another, for dealing with disagreement and for rational persuasion. By thirteen years in group discussion children can initiate, elicit, extend and qualify in a range of ways. These are called "collaborative moves" by Barnes & Todd (1977). For the thirteen year old there is a greater awareness of what other people might be thinking, which makes effective discussion easier. At the same time, since thirteen-year-olds are beginning to think more about what people are thinking about them, this awareness of self can be inhibiting. The spontaneity in language use which characterizes the middle school years is beginning to vanish as the emotional constraints of full adolescence begin to hinder it. Their *communicative competence*, already so well developed in many ways, can be hindered by an emotional maturity that in other ways is part of that competence. Before these emotional constraints become more dominant, children can be prompted towards more sustained levels of formal operational thinking by providing them with regular opportunities for dialogue with others, thereby laying the foundations for the *analytic competence* that they will need later in their schooling. Ability to think, as Moffett proposes, depends on the many previous dialogues people have taken part in.

There is then ample indication, from what we know about children's language and intellectual development in the middle school years, to guide and recommend educational approaches centred on using oral language. If these approaches are not put into practice in ordinary schools, it cannot be argued that failure to do so is due to any reservations about what children themselves at this stage can do with their oral language.

Conceptual development and schooling

The acquisition of concepts involves more than just getting some words to say. It means acquiring an interconnected set of words and connecting the meanings of these new words with others that we already have. We manage this process by talking and writing, in which we explain these new notions to ourselves. Reading on its own is rarely suffficient for conceptual development to proceed in the middle school. As I have stressed, mature concept formation from contextual material (i.e. from the pages of books) is only achieved at the earliest by the age of fifteen (Peel & de Silva, 1972). This means that conceptual development in the middle school years has to proceed along "experience-based" lines, using methods that are similar to those used in the first school, but more sophisticated. Shared experiences are needed; they have to be enjoyable and interesting; they have to be well-organized while still allowing children to express themselves naturally. Excursions, visits and practical work are a strong and wise feature of primary schooling, yet these features decline in importance in the early years of secondary schooling which are also the later middle school years. This failure at the early secondary level to provide experience from which conceptual development can proceed throws children back onto the more artificial methods of meaning acquisition, which research reported by Peel & de Silva suggests children are not ready for. The physical location of the secondary school, in practice, may prevent the widespread use of field studies and excursions, but there are vicarious approaches to experience-based work. These are introduced in a later section.

Whatever approaches are adopted, the key process in experience-based conceptual development is for the child to put a name to the experience. Children need the vital experience of an occasion for using a word or a phrase in a motivated way *for the very first time.* This prime occasion, in which they try out a concept and fit it into their repertoire, acts as a catalyst for further experience in using the word. It becomes itself a form of motivation. It is the very first tentative use of a word or phrase in speech which is the experience that matters.

Teachers presenting words to children and attempting to define them (in the manner discussed by Barnes, 1976) are avoiding their responsibility for children's conceptual development. Even where a topic can only be explored through secondary sources, away from the experience itself, there is a need for pre-adolescent children to talk over the concepts in groups and with the teacher, in order to evaluate and use what they find. Where technical words are insisted upon by teachers, without the prior experience of talk, children face two problems at once: organizing their thought and guessing what language is acceptable. In Barnes' view (1976), some able children can do this easily, but for others it closes off exploratory language use. If they have the prior experience of talk that uses the technical terms in a motivated way, children will rise to the teacher's hopes more often by using the terms and phrases in their formal work much more readily.

There is evidence now that many children, in school at least, do not readily use the vocabulary of the school (Corson, 1985). While most twelve-year-olds are unable to use many of the words of secondary education which fifteen-year-olds handle with ease, children of low-income families, whose life and language experiences may be narrower because of that low income, at twelve years seem to be at a particular disadvantage when compared with other children of the same age. One task of the school is to make the language of schooling a motivated part of the speech of its pupils, a part not despised or avoided in their everyday discourse. While still valuing the language children bring to school, the object of the school is to encourage the complete mastery of the language of their culture. Without this mastery children are denied power and influence over their own affairs, and an opportunity for success in education. The teachers' role in providing an unrestrained access to the language of the culture is much more than one of giving words to experience. They need to organize opportunities for words to be tried out by children in oral language, so that they can be fitted comfortably into children's active vocabularies. This comes most easily from an imaginative and ingenious use of the environment.

Using the environment

There is no doubt that children use language best in situations that are lively and relevant to them. Here are some examples of real situations around a school and the purposes served by using them:

- — planning the most interesting route for a class walk around a local area (solving a problem).
- — telling someone else how to use the overhead projector (sharing information).
- — listing suggestions through discussion for improvements to the

school playground (influencing others).
- taking part in a class council or school council meeting (getting things done).
- compiling instructions for using a class microscope (organizing the world around them).

Real situations for language use surround the school and teachers are limited only by the scope of their imaginations in using them. Small scale excursions offer many opportunities for children to talk with purpose. This is evidenced in the following description of the work of one group of Australian ten-year-olds (Education Department, 1982a,b). The occasion was a visit to an old churchyard to make rubbings from tombstones. During the excursion the children compared, speculated and predicted in oral language by:

- discussing unusual names (Ruby, Percival, etc.).
- wondering why so many children and babies died in those days.
- wondering what life was like 100 years ago.
- talking about the possible stories behind some of the inscriptions.
- discussing how the engraving was done, comparing different styles.
- swapping ghost stories and "when I was frightened" anecdotes.

Later, back at school, the same children displayed their rubbings and talked about them to others; brought along old tools and talked about those; read ghost stories and made a book of them; used role play to develop a drama set on a large farm, far from town, in the 1880s. Possible future directions for this class might include a visit to a colonial homestead, a convict settlement or a stonemason.

Where does the teacher come into all this experience-based talk? Apart from the obvious task of setting up the enterprise in the first place, the teacher's role increases in this kind of work, rather than the reverse. Connie Rosen (in Rosen & Rosen, 1973) believes that as children internalize verbal strategies they need the teacher's *direct* intervention less and less. The teacher sometimes introduces the theme and encourages new ways of exploring it; the teacher keeps it alive for sustained inquiry and concentration, by helping children to participate, not allowing them to be over-ruled by the more dominant, and letting the important contributions have time to settle; the teacher sets an example of how things may be discussed, interpreting children's meanings on occasions, and opening up all kinds of possibilities and explorations that they might otherwise miss. As children progress through their schooling, the teacher's task in this kind of activity is to become obsolete, to withdraw from centre stage.

The teachers' role in middle school oral language work

Changes in teacher attitudes are difficult to promote, yet in the area of oral language work changes seem so clearly needed. What are these changes? As a starting point we can use Barnes' point (1976) that teachers should begin to recognize oral language work in terms of *learning* rather than in terms of *performance*: motivated learning proceeds from talking in a structured context more surely than it does in the didactic situation of the teacher telling, provided that motivation is present in the talking context itself. This throws the responsibility back onto teachers to provide that motivation. The surest way of doing this may require another change in attitude on the part of teachers: they must begin to *value* the oral contributions of children, whether talking with them individually, in groups, or as whole classes. Most of all teachers must be attentive listeners, showing in their reception of pupils' oral contributions that they are taken seriously. In whole class discussions the teacher's example as a listener and valuer of talk is all important.

An extract from a whole class discussion, where a science teacher is working with a class of eleven-year-olds, is provided by Chilver & Gould (1982), who derive insights about teachers' roles in talk and the potential weaknesses of whole class discussions from their transcript. A major conclusion is that "difficult" classes have more chance of "achieving something" in group rather than whole class discussion. Yet the very nature of difficult classes tends to prevent teachers from vesting the trust in children that is necessary to encourage group work. Chilver & Gould further argue that the cohesion of a large group depends on the cohesion existing within the smaller groups of which it consists. Hence there is a real need for opportunities to work in small units prior to whole class discussion. Building upon this a skilled teacher can lead a discussion where winning and losing points is not important; where everyone is listened to; where there are no interruptions; and where no-one is made to feel foolish. Chilver & Gould lay stress upon an impersonality, a detachment, which is needed in the pursuit of knowledge-for-its-own-sake. On the other hand they warn that there may be an absence of genuine "involvement", which is a shortcoming that work with large oral groups invariably promotes. Listeners are not kept alert by the prospect of speaking themselves, since it is unnecessary to speak; listening levels decline; learning drops off. Chilver

& Gould suggest changes to the conventions of whole class discussion to make it more successful: encouraging talk rather than taking it over; playing the devil's advocate (adopting an opposing point of view for the sake of discussion); leaving the chair or the central role vacant; giving the chair to another. Most important of all they recommend that the teacher's role should provide a *model* of the conventions of good discussion and clear thinking.

With the basic requirement of an atmosphere of confidence and encouragement established, the next step for the teacher in whole class work is opening the discussion at the right moment and in the right way (see Britton in Barnes, Britton & Rosen, 1969). A tentative generalization offered (but not a string of them) is a good starting point. If this fails to elicit a response from the children, try another generalization contrasting with the first. If encouragement and confidence are present, pupil comments will begin to flow. Somewhere in these comments there will be a *question,* asked of the teacher by one of the children; this will turn the attention of the whole class to the teacher's reply in a way which exceeds in motivational possibilities *any* straight lecture situation. In being *asked* to talk, skilled teachers not only impart knowledge: they also become language models by using clear and well-formed sentences, as examples of language to be learned from. They also show from the context of their talk something about the meanings of the difficult words they use.

Early approaches in small group work require teachers to confirm for children their reliability as people to whom children can expose their thoughts and concerns with confidence (Lewis, 1979). Teachers' language will be a powerful model for children. By choosing words with care, sprinkling utterances sparingly and judiciously with concepts to be developed, teachers can encourage the children to use, "for the very first time" perhaps, new words representing the more difficult concepts of the task in hand. By carefully avoiding the "jargon of the school", and never using hard and long words only for effect, the teacher will encourage children to recognize that difficult words are *tools* of the language, nothing more: they help us to name distinctions and relationships, and by naming them they make them more readily available for use in thought and in the communication of meaning.

In evaluating the results of small group work teachers have several options: some discussions may be taped for later use, perhaps as a basis for discussion; the group might make notes and report back; or some longer written assignment might be required from the group or individual members. If the quality of group work is to be developed, teachers need feedback so that their attempts to improve the talk of groups can be informed.

Chilver & Gould suggest "factor" approaches to discussion as one technique for use with older middle school children: encouraging children to examine factors of different kinds (e.g. geographical, political, economic, military) which relate to a given problem. For example, the problem might be the serious matter of choosing a site for a new town in a distant colony (York in Canada for instance, later to become Toronto): various factors can be presented on work cards (drawn from the real historical instance) which the children can rank in importance and discuss as part of that ranking process. Another approach is for members to be asked to note points of disagreement and use these as the framework of a report. Teachers might also begin group discussion sessions with information sheets containing "new knowledge" to be integrated by children in terms of its relevance to an old problem. Once again, for example, having chosen a site for a colonial town, children could be moved forward a generation or two in time to discuss novel influences on the town which its founders could not have foreseen (for instance the nearness of York to a newly independent United States of America).

The teacher's choice of discussion "types and topics" will lead to different language functions being developed in the discussion, different aspects of communicative competence being developed. Work preparing speeches, a journalistic article or an improvised play will each promote a use of different registers and styles and will display the functional alternatives that language makes available. In the early middle school the teacher's presence in groups may be needed to establish some questioning patterns: "what's that for?" or "what do you think, John?". Staying too long, though, will provoke competition for the teacher's attention and change the style of exploratory language used so that it becomes a mere series of answers, not the reshaping of knowledge. The teacher's role is to provide a model of excellence: both as a sympathetic listener, and as a skilled user of language.

Classroom management

Class size is a major constraint on the amount of oral language work each child may receive in the middle school. Although the research on class size is inconclusive in recommending an optimum number of pupils, it is certain that classes employing discussion methods are constrained by pupil numbers. In the middle school I have found that a class of 24 children allows a use of five to six manageable groups in group teaching, and further allows for an *individualization of instruction*, the promotion of group dialogue and teacher-pupil discussion. Since individualization of instruction, as a thorough-going practice, is a relatively new notion in schooling, pleas for reduced class sizes from teachers have mainly gone unheeded. However, a synthesis of research evidence demonstrates that class size is strongly related to pupil achievement and that children in small classes have more interest in learning (Glass *et al.*, 1982).

Where subject-centred work is dominant and where children have different teachers for each subject area there is the risk of oral language being confined to "English" and not being used as a methodology "across the curriculum". The teacher intent on promoting oral language work really needs to be with a particular group or class for a good part of each day throughout the middle school years. Single teacher organization throughout the middle school years may not always be practical, but it is an ideal to be aimed at, even in the lower secondary years where the single class teacher, who knows the children, can reduce any anxieties in their oral language work that may arise, especially in improvisation, role play and whole class talk activities.

In many middle school classrooms talk is made easier by skilful and attractive partitioning, using trellises, draped fabrics, display boards and book cases. Without totally separating areas, there is a relative privacy and small groups can get on with their work (Rosen & Rosen, 1973). Oral work does mean noise. It usually means more than one person in a room talking at once. Co-operation with neighbouring classes to adjust timetables and to minimize disturbances is an act of professional courtesy which teachers will consider in their planning. Where the weather is fickle, there is even more reason to seize the moments of sunshine by going outside to work. It is worth adapting class schedules to capitalize on the moments of sunshine, since the children will be motivated by looking forward to these unscheduled periods of escape from the classroom, and oral work will benefit.

Approaches to oral language work

Whatever the subject area, there is room for an array of imaginatively organized talking situations, so that pupils can engage in talk to solve practical problems or to come to terms with complicated ideas. In this section I discuss approaches under four headings: 1) effective group talk or dialogue; 2) improvisation; 3) role play; and 4) reading aloud and storytelling. These are the most relevant approaches at the middle school level, although Chapter 5 contains other ideas that can be applied selectively in primary and lower secondary schooling.

Effective group talk or dialogue

Group dialogue in the middle school can be approached in two ways: by *group talk,* where the talk itself is the aim of the activity; or by *group discussion,* where the activity is directed towards a wider curriculum aim and is used as an instrument within a lesson's structure.

Group talk can be used in an open-ended syllabus where children identify areas of interest and issues which middle school teachers can build into their integrated curriculum planning. While not related specifically to any subject area, this activity still needs structure, since children will want to be clear about what they are supposed to be discussing. It can be a valuable approach within those areas of knowledge where matters of value and opinion limit the amount of "hard" knowledge that children can seize upon. Above all, it allows children to try on ideas and decide where they stand on important issues.

Group discussion is the most favoured approach in oral language work. Its demands on participants are much greater than those of group talk where perhaps only experience, memory and vocabulary are needed. In group discussions the child is called upon to theorize and generalize, to reason and formulate conclusions and decisions. Group discussion with eight- to ten-year-olds centres on manipulable material, where the answers to simple problems are available in the material used as a focus for the group: pictures, simple apparatus in science, the working of cameras or pocket calculators, the rules of simple games. There should be a direct connection, resident in the material, between the problems set for groups and the answers to these problems. There will be a need for whole class talk before and after the group discussion session. If this form of collaborative oral learning has not been used in the first school, discussion sessions should be short in duration at first, growing in length as more complex problems are presented.

With older middle schoolers one of the strengths of group discussion work is that it often confronts learners with viewpoints different from their own (Barnes & Todd, 1977). They come to see that there are many problems for which there is no one correct solution. By using group discussion, teachers communicate to children their belief in the value of talk in learning, and by holding follow-up discussions about discussions themselves they pass on explicitly their positive feelings about their talk. A relaxed familiarity with difficult concepts will develop if these are injected in whole class work before the discussion and if *work cards* focus on one or two new terms which children are invited to read and to use incidentally in their talk. Work cards provide an agenda for discussion

(Barnes & Todd, 1977). They eliminate the need for a "chairman", a role children find it difficult to cope with in any case. A tight series of questions, which helps to structure discussion but not predetermine its content, can be typed onto cards. One card is provided for each child. The type of question will vary. If pupils have a lot of everyday knowledge which is relevant, task questions will be looser. In science, for example, questions and instructions will be more direct and directing if explanations required are more removed from everyday ways of looking at things. An *open* approach, which encourages children to ask questions of one another, is the more profitable if "correct" answers to problems are not possible and if individual points of view are likely to conflict (Barnes, 1976).

Care in selecting groups for discussion work is essential. Groups of three to five members are the best arrangements. In my formal upper primary classes I used a sociometric test at the beginning of each term to decide group seating arrangements for everyday classwork. These groups would also become the networks for group discussion during the term's work. By asking children to indicate (confidentially on paper) their two closest friends in the class, it is an easy matter to plot a grouping arrangement where children have the security of someone in their group whom they are used to talking with. Older middle schoolers may prefer single-sex discussion groups. A sociometric test will reveal twelve and thirteen-year-olds choosing only members of their own sex as friends. There are other approaches to selecting groups. Chilver & Gould offer an approach using self-chosen groups, with the topic for the "assignment" itself determining group preferences.

Book discussion groups offer children the chance to become aware of story-telling styles and styles required for presenting information. Confidence in looking beyond the attractions of the covers of books and in the case of non-fiction judging how far it suits their purposes can be developed through discussion with their classmates; children learn to formulate for themselves what it is they enjoy and what they need to find out. In reading sets of books at the same pace and discussing them as they go, readers who are matched in reading ability can justify and adjust their understanding and interpretation of what they read. Discussions about books take a variety of forms but usually share common goals at the middle school level (Education Department, 1984):

— to give children the opportunity to talk in small groups;
— to encourage them to search for "shades of meaning" in their reading;
— to enable them to share their experience of the plot, the characters and the language of the book;

— to allow them to give voice to their attitudes, beliefs and understandings;
— to encourage careful listening;
— to help build and refine a personal value system for each child;
— to give each child the opportunity to see the world from different perspectives;
— to give children the chance to match situations in books with real life experiences and hopes;
— to provide a genuine teaching environment where the adult involved can address the key concerns of each one, giving insights about the more abstract meanings and the more complex values encountered.

From these aims it can be seen that children will at times be able to take responsibility for their own discussion groups and at other times some teacher or other adult can be brought into the groups to offer the enriching experiences suggested in the last of the aims. The following are some questions that can be used as starting points for book discussion groups:

— what is going on in the story or what is the passage about?
— what happened before this point in the story or how does this passage connect with what the reader already knows?
— what sort of story is this? what sort of people are these characters? what sort of information is this?
— what could be expected to happen next? (in non-fiction) where is this information going or what is the next topic likely to be?
— was the reader's earlier expectation justified and if not where did the reader or the group go astray in building expectations?

Fry (1985) devotes a complete study to children talking about books. He concludes that by encouraging talk of this kind we are helping children to reflect upon themselves as readers and upon what happens as they read.

By the final years of middle schooling, if group discussion has been a progressively developed feature of their work, thirteen-year-olds will think nothing of moving into groups to reflect verbally on some aspect of the curriculum. At this age, without the teacher's presence, children can control their progress in discussion, deal with competition and conflict, provide supportive behaviour for one another and collaborate in reaching an endpoint and defend that conclusion (Barnes & Todd, 1977).

Improvisation

Improvisation activities can generate a rich and varied range of oral language. Put simply, an improvisation is a play without a script. In preparing for improvisation work, children again work in groups, allotting characters in their discussion, and deciding how they can best reveal their insights into the story they intend to represent in the improvisation. Improvisation as a pedagogy for learning within subjects provides the direct experiences necessary for further learning and vicarious representations of events which cannot be brought into the classroom in any other way (Mallett & Newsome, 1977).

Subject matter for improvisation can be drawn from any of the curriculum knowledge areas. Taking a known story and inventing an imagined variation of it is a favoured method that is recommended and discussed in Mallett & Newsome (1977). Self (1976) suggests teaching aids for this kind of work and discusses the problem of noise level. Britton (1970) sees in the world of myth and faery a rich source of improvisation material; he suggests that talking, writing, reading, painting, movement, model-making and music-making all contribute to improvisation and are generated by it.

Perseverance on the part of the teacher is required, though. If a single attempt to dramatize a history lesson fails, it is too easy to despair of the approach. The process becomes easier with every attempt. As a beginning to improvisation work, a programme for a single term's work was used in my upper primary classes, modelled on suggestions in Way's book (1967) *Development Through Drama.* This book remains a standard teacher's guide in this area.

Role play

In child drama work, in the early years of the middle school, children will adopt characters of the fantasy or imaginative world. Gradually, and parallel with the children's growth in awareness of the world around them, the characters of the real world begin to attract their interest. This development is not regular and it is slow, but like the onset of formal operational thinking the process can reach towards a full changeover in the last years of the middle school. Role play is an activity for these later years of middle schooling. Its links with the development of communicative competence are obvious ones. Role play is an aid to honesty, since the children engaged in a role play situation, which they accept as real, become emotionally as well as rationally involved (Phillips *et al.*, 1970). Insight and learning become possible for the group involved, while an audience witnessing the role play is equipped with a three dimensional basis for viewing the issue presented and for informing later discussion. Self (1976) deals extensively with role play across the curriculum; he provides a specimen "syllabus" for use at the middle school level.

Reading aloud and storytelling

Both of these must be pleasurable activities. The essential requirement for both is a willing audience. Reading-around-the-class, a common strategy not long ago in schools, ignored this requirement for a willing audience and motivation often disappeared from the situation as a result. As with all language development, the question of audience and purpose affects performance in reading aloud. Reading aloud can be part of classroom activities in a number of ways. Children can read aloud:

— to share stories or information;
— to obtain help in understanding;
— to get new ideas;
— to give support to some viewpoint they wish to express.

Because reading is a complex process, the reader needs to be given a fair opportunity to prepare any passage before reading it aloud. The chosen passage should also have a unity and coherence which helps the reader and the listener; this will help bridge the distance between the reader and the audience and encourage the reader to put meaning and confidence into the presentation. At different times and for different reasons children can read to individuals in their class, small groups, the whole class, other classes and interested adults who enjoy children's company.

The adult model of the good reader is important: children benefit from hearing adults read for a wide variety of purposes, including stories, discussing information, checking ideas and details, reading maps and diagrams and reading signs and instructions.

Reading in groups of comparable fluency, with children prepared in advance, having checked to see that they understand what they are to read, is a recommended approach. Doubly valuable is for children to read their own written work aloud to other children, since the prospect of an audience will motivate both the writing and the reading.

In telling or retelling stories (Reed, 1976) children use many functions of language: narrating, describing, sequencing, explaining. By demanding explicitness (that is, recreating in the present in words a context which is absent), this approach bridges the language of school and everyday language. Storytelling is a significant element in everyday communication, in the communicative competencies of articulate adults. Children's self-esteem can be improved if the school helps them to master the techniques required, since an ability to tell jokes, to reminisce, to relate anecdotes — the skills of a raconteur — is prized and envied. Storytelling is also good for the listeners because they are brought to visualize and project, and to interpret a logical sequence of events.

Oral language across the middle school curriculum

My division of the curriculum of the middle school below is not an arbitrary one. It attempts to follow in a logical way philosophical discussion on what "forms of knowledge" might be represented in the school curriculum. I attempt to conform to the forms of knowledge identified by Hirst (1974), not because that curricular mapping system is the only one available to us, but because it has become the most influential. Teachers need to be in tune, as well, with the serious problems that arise in defending any single "forms of knowledge" approach to the curriculum; for example, there is no hard and fast way of deciding where many knowledge categories begin and where others end. Ideas of this kind have been used to argue the case for a greater degree of *subject integration* across the curriculum. There is certainly methodological advantage for my task here, however, in seeing the curriculum as a set of component knowledge areas rather than as some holistic entity.

The five sub-sections below are: 1) the humanities (human science/social studies); 2) expressive arts, creative arts and human movement; 3) mathematics; 4) values education; and 5) the natural world. They represent integrated knowledge categories that are distinct from one another to the extent that each one asks us to look at the world from a slightly different perspective, but they are similar to one another in that they are all interpreted through language, and may be readily approached as forms of knowledge through oral language.

By not including "English" or "Language Arts" as a separate category, I am not just conforming to the view that "mother tongue" is not a separate knowledge category. My purpose here is to show how language integrates across the curriculum. The isolated place of "English" in the curriculum may be somewhat miseducative. I have already pointed out in Chapter 1 how a misunderstanding about the doctrine of "language across the curriculum" arises from the wrong belief that responsibility for that doctrine mainly or even especially rests with teachers of English. Schooling in "language" might be better without the presence of a separate subject called "English", whose very existence may discourage in other subjects a use of strategies that should inform all subjects.

The humanities [human sciences/social studies]

A judicious blend of whole class teaching and group work in the Humanities is a common pattern that can be followed throughout the middle school years. In discussion groups children are asked to share their wisdom, discoveries and knowledge; they are urged to formulate questions to which the group can then find answers; and they are required to report back and to justify their activities to other class members.

Discussion group work is used as a precursor to written work (Barnes, 1976). Ideas are inter-related and given new meanings in relation to specific questions presented to groups by their teachers. Value systems, children's feelings and attitudes are brought to the surface in discussion and the subject matter of the humanities is seen to be more than an accumulation of facts, dates and places.

Children in the middle school do not always find it easy to think realistically about a way of life which is not their own. Discussion work allows them to talk their way into insights about the topic. As useful, in dealing with the more remote or exotic topics, is improvisation work and role play. In role play children can be presented with a real-life problem in outline, perhaps drawn from an everyday crisis faced by people in another culture. A role play exercise, prepared in discussion groups, will bring out the human issues which affect decision-making, and confront children with problems which can then be related to their own world. Individual written work, after an exercise of this kind, will show the benefit of new insights and will lead to a motivated use of expressive language.

A humanities curriculum centred on a broad theme of "human beings and their environment" is found to be appropriate in many upper middle schools. An integrating idea of this kind allows the links between subjects to be displayed. Oral language can be the chief medium of this integration in a curriculum. The "links" between subjects (such as those between English, History and Geography) are recognized as too important to be omitted from a central place in the curriculum. We may give order to our curriculum by calling the overall integration of subjects "Humanities" or "Human Sciences" or "Social Studies". The general title is less important, however, than displaying the integration between the subject areas to the children, since the many points of integration are centres of considerable appeal in the real world of the child (for example, a market place, a railway station, an eskimo village, etc.). Discussion group work, in the middle school, is a chief method for demonstrating these points of integration to children. It allows them to see the various subject areas as components in a single "knowledge area" which has the features of an interconnected whole and which we describe with some accuracy as the "human sciences". Within discussion groups children are asked to share their wisdom, discoveries and knowledge; they are uged to formulate questions to which the group can then find answers; and they are required to report back and to justify their activities to other class members. Because middle school children have no preconceived ideas on what makes a subject, and because they tend to hold abstract notions like "subjects" in a fairly volatile way, *all* of their experiences, *across* the many subject boundaries, are available for inclusion as the content of the discussion. The teacher's role becomes one of challenging the discussion with issues and materials which will promote a consideration of information from all those subjects that are to be integrated.

A detailed and integrated Humanities programme is discussed in a Schools Council Working Paper (Mallett & Newsome, 1977). This programme uses group discussion work as its main methodology. It provides a scheme for two years' work, with each of the following topics representing a single term's work:

1. the structure of the earth/prehistory;
2. our land in prehistory; how humans survive; language and communication;
3. the medieval world;
4. ancient civilizations: Greece and Rome;
5. the Renaissance and exploration;
6. agriculture and village life.

Expressive arts, creative arts and human movement

Physical games and oral language, music and movement, song and poetry, improvisation and fictional narrative, all form natural pairs. Activities initiated in one area can become the basis for dramatic improvisation; music can be created to accompany a dramatic scene; language activities can provide the rule structure for games; and creative poetry making and writing can follow group discussions where children structure knowledge and express a wide range of feelings. Ideas for middle school work linking music, literature and drama are presented in Mallett & Newsome (1977).

The role of oral language in art activities for children can be shown through an example (Education Department, 1985). After an excursion to a gorge, a teacher and her grade 6 class recalled the turbulent water in the river and the feelings as they walked across the bridge. Some children spoke of the steep uphill slope in the path and of their tiredness in the heat; others spoke of the peacocks they had seen; others of the feathers they had collected; others of the sounds they had heard above the noise of the water. Each group then worked in either sound or movement to recreate or symbolize some aspect of the excursion. Through talk and recall each group came to a decision about the focus they would select. In several groups there was further discussion, argument, anecdotal talk, speculation, questioning, planning and decision-making as the children experimented with sound or movement, selected, sequenced and refined their work. Recent research (Parsons *et al.*, 1984) suggests that the most valuable opportunities for using expressive and evaluative talk occur as children reflect on the work they have carried out. Often the teacher can take part in this discussion by encouraging the children:

— to consider reasons for their opinions: "why do you think that?"
— to reconsider their attitudes: "how do you think another might feel?"
— to speculate and imagine: "what would happen if . . .?"
— to evaluate: "do things like that happen to people?" etc.

Music making activities, in which children are encouraged to experiment with vocal sounds, are very valuable in making them aware of their voices as expressive instruments. Useful sound-making activities to help children over their initial embarrassment include simple sound stories using voices and body sounds (for example, the sounds heard at a fairground). More complex activities may include the development of simple individual sound patterns, initially orchestrated by the teacher and later by a child in the group, either randomly or to develop a predetermined pattern. One patterned sequence, for example, might bring in individual sound patterns one after another in a cumulative effect, then drop them out one by one until only one is left. Variations can be added, such as working toward or away from a climax. Other activities may use voices to produce sound sequences that express a mood or atmosphere. Children may weave words, phrases or even brief poems into such sequences. As they work together in music-making activities, children make decisions, discuss and evaluate ideas and interact socially. They are using language for a multitude of purposes.

In visual arts, when working together to complete a group project, children also use language for many purposes. In one class three boys working together on a box construction were heard to use language to solve problems, to speculate, to criticize, to support, to question, to recall and to compare (Education Department, 1985). Here is part of this conversation:

> She said a metre . . .
> A metre's about there . . .
> It has to be tall, doesn't it?
> Yeah, a metre high, not wide.
> This could make an arch, couldn't it?
> So people could climb up into it . . .
> And this could stick out here . . .
> If that was an arch . . . Hey leave it alone, you'll tear it!
> Wait a minute . . . [puts box on top]
> Yeah . . . that looks good.
> Better get the scissors . . .
> Hey, you want to swap for this?
> You can have the other one.
> Then see . . . you could paint it here . . . inside . . . then you'd see inside through the arch.
> Now we've got to do this arch . . .
> That's really tricky . . .
> Aw, just go for it!
> No! You'll spoil it!
> You only want the shape of the arch . . . let's just paint it on?
> Then it won't be high enough!
> Put this on top then.

Not all types of drama activity are equally effective in creating opportunities for children's language development (Parsons *et al.*, 1984). Presentational drama in which the children make up short scenes to perform to others employs a restricted range of language uses. The fact that the scene is to be shown to others becomes more important to the children than any exploration of the ideas being presented. The resulting drama is often superficial and stereotyped. If this is the only kind of drama that children meet they are not being extended in either their thinking or their use of language. An ability to communicate ideas to others, rather than merely to act out a series of events, develops with maturity and after considerable experience of a wide variety of drama.

Whole class drama, in which no attempt is made to communicate to others outside the drama, gives richer opportunities to explore attitudes and the meaning of events from within a fictional situation. Often this kind of drama involves the teacher taking an active role within the drama, by challenging children to think more realistically about attitudes and assumptions they have made, by helping them persevere with the task, and by asking them to justify actions and roles that they take. Teacher and children may interact as;

— workers and management;
— residents and local authorities;
— members of a family;
— subjects and ruler;
— members of a community;
— crew and captain on a ship or spaceship;
— social workers and elderly people.

Using these and an array of variations that are possible, many contexts for drama can be explored and various degrees of formality and informality in relationships can be experienced. Communicative competence grows. Aspects of power, authority and prejudices to be found within societies can be experienced imaginatively and later discussed.

Drama arouses children's curiosity and often sends them to the library shelves to find out more about people or issues raised in the drama. It can be structured so that children are given opportunities to gain experience in using particular kinds of language, to use an unfamiliar vocabulary and to use language appropriate to a range of social situations. Some children may experience for the very first time a deliberate use of language to speculate, to identify problems, to consider alternatives, to give logical reasons, to elaborate a place or scene, or to use a style of language appropriate to a special situation.

Mathematics

It is important not to draw artificial links between mathematics and oral language work. Most of the children's time in Maths is spent in puzzling out problems on their own, working with pen and paper. However, in the middle school the foundations for conceptual development in Maths are laid; new concepts are best acquired by trying out the names of the concepts in motivated language. Observation confirms that middle schoolers often do not begin to understand the concepts teachers use in Maths until years after they are first introduced. Sometimes the concepts are never fully grasped and the child in confusion turns away from mathematics as a result. Group work in the early years, with talk centred on manipulable materials, will bring children to use and to begin to see the important (but apparently pointless) differences between such terms as ratio and percentage, fraction and decimal, sum and product. The motivation of group work, centred on an interesting activity, will provoke a use of specialist terminology, especially where vertical grouping (children of different ages) and mixed ability arrangements provide children with the language model of another child more advanced in conceptual development.

Measurement exercises are a central feature of middle school Maths and these are best approached in group work, with activity cards and measuring apparatus for quantity, volume, weight and length available to groups (Martin *et al.,* 1976). A concept like "probability" cannot be conveyed in the teacher's words. The teacher will certainly have hard knowledge about probability to convey but it may be meaningless if children have not worked in groups first with dice, pennies or roulette wheels, seeing for themselves in their talk around the activities that probability is a notion worth thinking and talking about.

Role play activities, similar to those discussed earlier in this chapter, can be used to bring Maths and the real world a little closer, especially where real world conflicts over money matters or aspects of home building are used as the basis of the role play. A middle school class teacher, who is responsible for the children's whole day at school, will be able to integrate Maths with other subjects where group discussion is more prominent. Constructing time lines and charts in the Humanities calls for a high level application of mathematical understanding, as does a use of maps and weather charts. Co-operative group talk will motivate children towards expanding their competence. Group survey work based on interviews and the compilation of statistics will help children to discover the kind of information they can acquire through asking questions. By learning how to frame questions in this way, younger middle schoolers build up the competence they need for talking in the absence of the teacher and for taking part in genuine discussion in a large group.

Values education

This curriculum area incorporates the knowledge categories of moral understanding, religious studies and the introductory elements of philosophy (such as logical sequencing, showing equivalence, contradicting, reaching conclusions and inferring). Role play, improvisation, social drama, whole class discussion and especially small group discussion are valuable methodologies in teaching about values.

Moral education is not concerned with deciding "rightness". Its concern is with the process of moral decision-making: how is "rightness" to be decided? It aims to encourage in children a concern for reflection *before* action in any situation where values need to be taken into account. This asks the moral decision-maker to consider the viewpoints of others. Others' viewpoints need to be at least recognized, and preferably understood. In small group discussion, where resolving a simple moral dilemma provides the topic for talk, older middle school children can be encouraged to say, in certain circumstances, what they *ought* to do, rather than just what they *would* do. Analytic competence is developing.

The process of moral development is a slow one, following it seems similar developmental stages to intellectual development, but there is little doubt that the process can be accelerated if children are brought to consider and discuss the taking of moral decisions as a regular part of their classroom work. This is partly because there are strong links between moral reasoning and language development. There is now a common view (Siegal, 1975) that since language comprehension plays a central role in conceptual development, the fact that moral language is difficult to learn results in problems for moral conceptual development.

Social drama is a combination of improvisation and role play. The mastery of a situation from a number of viewpoints is more readily achieved through practice than through mere verbal instruction. For example, a small role play might be devised by children in which a group of friends tease a strange child about his appearance. Each member could take turns in playing the various roles and "trying on the feelings" that are relevant. Discussion, after the social drama, is the point at which the teacher can integrate the issues and values involved, perhaps later sending children into groups to discuss a further social situation, which is a variation on the one used in the improvisation. Self (1976) and Way (1967) suggest topics and approaches in this area.

In Religious Studies, as in the Humanities, there is wide scope for improvisation, following on from some wider work examining religious practices and stories which occur outside our immediate culture. Improvisation work can make the necessary connection between religion and values a plain one for children: by being asked to improvise a variety of religious stories from various cultures, children may come to see that religion can influence values for good or ill.

Finally there is a very practical application of "talk" in school and classroom "values" management. In short group discussions, school rules can be examined, and class rules can be *decided*. From groups reporting back on their findings class rules, remarkably similar to the teacher's wishes, can be framed. Children will more readily conform to these rules since they have had a say in deciding them.

The natural world

In the sciences, as in mathematics, the technical language of the subjects can be a most intimidating obstacle for young children. Their grasp of specialist concepts can determine, in the long run, their success. During experimental work in the science lesson, encourage children to talk amongst themselves, allowing, too, a certain amount of social chatting (Schools Council, 1980). In the middle school the interests of children focus, after a while, on the present, and social chatting will eventually centre on the job-in-hand: "what are you doing?", "how did that happen?", "what's the name of this stuff?". In whole class talk, preliminary to experimental work or where teachers perform experiments, they can collect all kinds of opinions, both right and wrong, before getting around to the closest solution to a problem (Barnes, Britton & Rosen, 1969).

In group discussion work in science the work card is essential. If work cards call for explanations rather than right or wrong answers, discussion will benefit and so will learning. Work cards can be designed to encourage children to go beyond the tasks planned by the teacher. Barnes (1976) reviews a programme of work in environmental studies that is suited to upper middle schoolers and incorporates a wide use of group talk. Barnes is very critical of the word-teaching practices, commonly used in the sciences in particular, where "presentation" of the "technical terms" by teachers is thought to be sufficient to *establish* the concept for children. Conceptual learning, though, does not arise merely through "having the word"; a technical term must be inserted firmly into the related ideas and terminology of a realm of discourse by children if it is to have permanence and significance for them. This form of word-learning comes most readily not through teaching but through effective talk around the subject matter that embeds the concept.

In science discussion sessions, the meanings of new words receive a lot of attention from children. They are keen to get meanings right, to work them out and to use them in their own utterances in the discussion. Chilver & Gould present an extract from a discussion of a passage in a text by a group of eleven-year-olds. Their task in this discussion is to take a complex passage, about the temperature of the sun, read it, talk about any difficulties and agree on its main points. Their frequent questioning of each other is a striking feature of the discussion: learning is proceeding. Disputation and the refining of ideas clearly leads to a better understanding of the text; each one brings relevant knowledge and commonsense views to the discussion. There are weaknesses, too, in the discussion: there is an absence of precision; one member dominates too often; and another member is too little involved. Chilver & Gould list some initiatives that the attentive teacher can take to provide models for better group work across the curriculum: organizing changes in group membership; encouraging talk about the discussion process itself; and illustrating alternative styles of discussion.

An oral language policy for the middle years

I have already introduced the topic of school language policies in Chapter 1. Strictly speaking, the subject is outside the scope of a book such as this intended for individual classroom practitioners. Since "language across the curriculum" is by definition outside the range of control of any one teacher who is confined to a single class level or curriculum area, it becomes by default the responsibility of the school executive; the design of language policies is a task of educational administration. Nevertheless, I have included here a working example of the kinds of prescriptions that can be made in formulating an oral language policy across the curriculum (Anderson, 1986). This may be useful for beginning teachers at the middle school level who want to see how the ideas outlined in this chapter can be brought together in a practical situation where language is formally recognized as fundamental to learning and as the key to intellectual development. In general a school language policy should provide major guidelines for action; it should create a framework that allows discretion, yet provides direction:

A Kindergarten to Form Six Oral Language Policy

1. We shall provide the widest possible range of learning situations that will require many different ways of speaking.
2. We shall offer patterns of work that will depend upon the collaboration of several members of a class and the active participation of the teacher in the role of experienced user of language.
3. We shall plan the social contexts of our classrooms to take account of the way in which human beings develop a command of language.
4. At all grade levels and in all subjects we shall make room for talk, so that children can solve their own practical problems and come to terms with complicated ideas.

5. We shall promote oral language in the classroom through:

group discussion	drama
improvisation	art activities
role play	music
whole class drama	poetry reading
excursions	telling and retelling stories

6. We shall provide an atmosphere of trust and respect in our classrooms that encourages talk: by listening to the children, by valuing the oral contributions that they offer, by making time for conversation and dialogue, and by giving them something real to talk about.

7. As teachers we shall encourage children to think and talk about:
   what is happening
   what happened
   what always happens
   what might happen
   why things might happen
   what if

8. We shall place stress on encouraging a use of the following thought processes through children's language activities, from an early age:
   identifying
   sequencing
   categorizing
   hypothesising
   imagining

9. We shall encourage children to generate their own hypotheses, beginning with speculation about the concrete world and then moving later towards abstraction.

10. Through their questioning teachers will promote children's ability to identify, sequence, classify, etc. and will use every one-to-one encounter during the day as an opportunity for talk and the development of language.

11. Records will be kept: to show the kinds of situations provided for each class that enabled children to extend and refine their use of language; and to provide an evaluation of each child's communicative competence.

Summary

The middle school years are a distinct language development stage. The process of intellectual development can be accelerated by oral language work. Children internalize the product of their dialogue and allow it to influence their thinking and future talk. Our thinking prowess depends on the many former dialogues we have taken part in.

If oral language approaches are not put into practice in ordinary schools, this failure cannot be excused by any reservations we might have about what children themselves at this stage can do with their oral language. The teacher's role in conceptual development is to encourage and organize opportunities for words and phrases to be tried out by children in oral language, so that they can be fitted readily into children's active vocabularies and become available as tools for thought.

Group discussion, group talk, improvisation, role play, reading aloud and storytelling are oral language approaches that can be used as methods across the middle school curriculum. The teacher's role grows in importance in oral language work. The skilful incorporation of talk is possible in any middle school subject where pupils meet problems that can be solved by talking them over until they see possible solutions.

5 Oral language in the senior secondary school

Very often the use of talk in school work decreases for children as they enter the senior years. Teachers are pushed by the curriculum demands of formal examinations to concentrate on didactic teaching styles; there is also pressure to focus more on literacy and literary skills and to disregard the adolescent's well-developed flair for learning through oral language. Yet few experienced teachers of adolescents would disagree with Britton's judgement (1970:223):

> "Perhaps the most important general implication for teaching, however, is to note that anyone who succeeded in outlawing talk in the classroom would have outlawed life for the adolescent: the web of human relations must be spun in school as well as out."

Because the oral skills of children from fourteen years onwards are very close to those of adults, the need to develop these skills further seems less urgent. It is true that by this stage of schooling teachers are aiming to do much more than develop the basic skills of literacy, numeracy and spoken language. They are attempting to find pedagogies to facilitate the learning process and the acquisition of knowledge by pupils. Oral language work, at a time when children are beginning to discover and use their capacity for analytical conversation, provides a key pedagogy for the senior school curriculum. If we agree with Britton's view above, the motivation necessary for successfully using the methodology is present in adolescent children already. The justification for its use has been part of educational doctrine at least since the Newbolt Report in 1921, which claimed that the only way to get a child to think about knowledge "is to get him to talk about it". What remains is for the pedagogy to be applied in classwork by teachers who are familiar with suitable approaches to oral work and with its contribution to analytic competence.

This chapter introduces suitable approaches for use across the curriculum in the senior grades. It needs to be read in conjunction with the previous chapter, "Oral Language in the Middle School". Approaches discussed in that chapter have application in senior secondary schooling as well as in the middle school. Discussion in this chapter is directed more to those techniques that can be added to that earlier repertoire of approaches; the range of methods grows because of the acceleration in linguistic and intellectual development that occurs in later adolescence.

Language and intellectual development in adolescence

By fourteen years many adolescents begin to show a preference and a capacity to reason more by means of verbally stated hypotheses and less by using language centred on the manipulation of and the relationships between concrete objects. They show a desire in their thinking to proceed logically from what is possible to what is empirically real: this allows them to develop theories about the world that may be far removed from the world as they perceive it. This stage of development opens up a range of abilities to the child: to imagine hypothetical possibilities; to consider in an exhaustive way the various combinations of events that might occur; to reason in a logical fashion; to handle certain types of scientific problem solving; to speak about theories of society or of religion; and to engage in advanced forms of moral judgement. Central to this process is the establishment in the mind of ideas, drawn from the culture, that link up as fairly permanent concepts for them. Adolescents are becoming familiar with the patterns of meanings in their society and culture that they must acquire to function with ease and independence within that society and culture.

The transcript of speech, below, is from a fifteen year old comprehensive school girl from South Yorkshire. Fiona is from an upper middle class background; she is of average reasoning ability for her age and has had a school experience that is fairly typical for children living in her region. She is replying, in conversation, to questions that invite her to use language in at least two different ways: to describe and to explain. This transcript and the others that follow are taken from studies in the sociology of language examining the lexical range of secondary school children from various social group backgrounds (Corson, 1985):

1. *Would you tell me about the teachers at that last school of yours?*
. . . Mrs L. was OK . . . I don't think she put too much into the children. She didn't really sort of . . . try to understand . . . she didn't try to . . . get into . . . the problems. She was a bit of a surface teacher. She didn't sort of

attempt to get any, lower into the real problems. She just either dismissed them as good, bad and indifferent. You know . . . I wasn't too bothered about the teacher, Mrs L. I think she would distance people . . . One or two people who were hard done by her. She didn't get very involved . . . I had better teachers before that, apart from that.

2. *What sort of person would you describe as a good person?*
Somebody who knows when to be honest. And to tell the truth. And . . . Somebody who's tactful. Doesn't tell whatever you say to somebody else. Who is, well, if it's important it means something to you. Knows how to keep a secret . . . Somebody who's kind and nice . . . Kind to animals, younger people.

3. *Would you say that telling a lie is always wrong?*
No. There are some cases, obviously, when the truth is more hurtful, I think. You shouldn't want to hurt people. Well, I don't mean that . . . I mean hurting really badly . . . for instance . . . well, there are some people who can't cope with the truth. Just have to tell them lies then. Little lies, I don't mean anything really big.

4. *When would it not be wrong?*
Well, if something was really wrong with somebody. A really . . . disease that was going to kill them. Something like that. They weren't capable of coping with that sort of a thing. Collapsed or . . . mental collapse sort of. Kind of thing. If truth would really hurt somebody.

5. *What about killing; would you say that killing another person is always wrong?*
No. I have sympathy, I have sympathy with mercy killing . . . People who kill other people who have cancer or things like that. But I don't think that really qualifies as killing. Yes. In the general case I think that killing's wrong . . . Nobody has the right to kill another person, anything. Everything has the right to live.

6. *When would it be all right to kill another person?*
If other people . . . if say, they had a disease, something like cancer or something and you really knew it was going in the end . . . kill them in any case and they were just going to go through an awful lot of suffering, I think that that would be right. But I think you don't kill somebody without the consent of the person concerned . . . Not necessarily, well, if they were adult enough and capable of coping with it . . .

7. *Are there any things that it is always wrong to do?*
Provoke people . . . tease them . . . push them . . . get at them . . . Mental bullying . . . that's very wrong. It is a form of bullying of course. Physical,

after you've got over it it's ok, but, to do that sort of scars your mind in a way . . . I think that sums it up. Picking on somebody smaller than you or, or less capable than you. At least your physical size doesn't matter so much, bullying in that way. Any sort of picking on people I can't stand that.

8. *If you could choose the laws by which we live which new ones would you choose?*
The existing ones? I'd make an offence, steal and . . . obvious things like that, you know. It's it is necessary to . . . to abide by your code, because otherwise you just wouldn't have civilization without . . . a society, and it's very important we have a society that works together, so laws that would draw the society together, and not let them become divided.

Fiona's answers to these questions are very like the kinds of answers young adults would give. Her speech is littered with "difficult" words, especially ones that relate to various mental states and social relationships. Her language displays an adult-like precision in using these difficult concepts; indeed the way she uses the words confirms that she grasps these difficult concepts very well indeed. Look for example at her elaboration of the meaning of "surface teacher" in question 1. and her clarification of the meaning of "mercy killing" in 5. Her use of difficult words is accompanied by a use of complex sentence structures; these allow her to express her real personal meanings succinctly and convincingly ("capable of coping with it"; "physical size doesn't matter so much"; "laws that would draw the society together"). Her language gives us clues about the sorts of oral language tasks that we can profitably present to older adolescents. On the evidence of Fiona's talk, we can ask them to theorize objectively, to handle abstract concepts with due regard for their logical relationships, and to apply these to new concrete situations that must be viewed in abstract terms.

Fiona shows keen insight into the feelings of others, their motives, their weaknesses, their fears, their sensitivities. More than this, she expresses these insights with ease and she clearly *wants* to talk about them. She manages to "get inside" others rather well; she has a capacity to analyse things that she finds hard to suppress. Look at question 1: even when the point of the question could be met by a straightforward descriptive response, she is drawn into analysis: her *analytical competence* in verbal thought betrays itself in her outward language. Elsewhere too she displays the older adolescent's "intoxication with logic" (Boden, 1979); there is less of a tendency towards the dogmatism, characteristic of younger adolescents, which I pointed to in a transcript in Chapter 4. Fiona does have strong opinions, but they are not dogmatically expressed. She uses modifying adverbs, expressions of doubt, hypotheticals and the conditional mood. For example she says "in some cases", "for instance", "in the general case", "if, say, they had a disease". Above all she intimates that life, for herself as an adolescent, is more concerned with solving human problems and coping with uncertainty than it is with merely doing things. She has moved in her interests well into the world of ideas: the ability to handle difficult concepts in thought is central to this engagement with the abstract world.

What follows on pages 96 to 98 are transcripts of a different kind: they are oral texts from fifteen-year-olds who learned English, in Australia, as their second language. These are included for two reasons: they give further support to the claims that I have made about adolescent levels of intellectual and linguistic development; and they offer compelling evidence of the benefits to intellectual functioning that a history of rich oral language experiences can bring to children.

These two fifteen-year-olds represent some 30 adolescents from immigrant backgrounds interviewed and taped at one school. On their arrival in their working class primary school (their former school) as five-year-olds none of the children knew English. The majority were from Yugoslavian, Italian or Portuguese family backgrounds; the languages of their parents' homelands were the languages of their home environments and to a great extent the languages of their Australian neighbourhoods as well.

These immigrant children were placed in classes that included indigenous Anglo-Australian children who were also from low-income backgrounds. They were given an intensive ESL (English as a Second Language) education, on a withdrawal basis, throughout their early years of schooling. This ESL education was provided in small groups, following the fairly structured and prescriptive materials popular in the early 1970's, but centred on the oral use of language through experience-based conversation with the teacher and participation in question-and-answer group talking. No teaching was conducted in their first languages since bilingual schooling, as a serious doctrine in Australian education, had not appeared at that time. After leaving the infant section of the school, the oral English of these children was found to be proficient enough not to need any further deliberate attention. Although they were behind their peers in written language, special language help was rarely needed in the primary years. They were exposed in their primary years to a language-based-curriculum introduced as a policy for the whole school and aimed deliberately at vocabulary development in all children. In measures of their language at fifteen years and in their year 10 school assessments these immigrant children, as a group, far exceeded their Anglo-Australian poorer working class peers, who had attended the same schools and were matched with them in their non-verbal reasoning skills. The two abbreviated oral transcripts below reveal this language skill at work.

Rozita is a fifteen year old whose first language is Macedonian:

1. *I'm very interested in schools here in Wollongong. Would you tell me all about that last school of yours?*
Well my last school. It's a very old school. It's been here, it was built in 1862 as far as I can remember . . . Oh, it's very old as I said and the school, in there school is really different to what it is to now, to High Schools. Like in primary you're used to using all simple things whereas, I had to myself adapt to something more difficult in High School. Whereas in primary all we, all you were used to doing is . . . the teacher would help you as much as she can and you weren't sort of pushed to, to do, to be doing things whereas here, like you're working your time is faster. You got to be working very quick and . . .

2. *What did you enjoy most about that school?*
The library. I really enjoyed the library. I was library monitor there. I really loved dealing with books and people. I really liked the library; 'Cause I spend most of my time there anyway . . .

3. *What did you dislike about that school?*
What I disliked about the school was the toilets. They weren't very, well, they were very messy and dirty. Not many people use them the way they're supposed to use them. In that, I mean very unclean. And the playgrounds. They were very rocky and dirty. They weren't like, now they've got concrete it's much easier for the children to play, whereas before they only had grass and everything and dirt and we used to always get . . . when it was windy, all the stone; and also another disadvantage with that school is we're near the steelworks. And when they used to let out the smoke it used to go all over the school and and we were, yeah, we were sent, we were asked to be, to go into the school because of that pollution. And a year ago, I think it was that, all the children had to be tested for lead in their blood. That was very bad. I, that's one big disadvantage. I think many people do agree with that. Near the pollution; and this does happen every day. All the kids have to put up with it.

4. *Would you say that killing another person is always wrong?*
It's always wrong. I think it would, it would be wrong to take somebody's life. Why should you take their life? I mean you sort of kill them, can't always settle something by killing them. Like if they say . . . if they did something against you, you don't go off and kill them just because they did

something against you. You can sort it out like humans. Sit down and talk over it, or, if it was a criminal case, you'd take 'em to court, I suppose. You don't kill them. Why should you take somebody's, else, somebody else's life. I mean that's pretty far-fetched. I think anyway.

5. *If you could choose the laws by which we live which new ones would you choose?*
A new law . . . I was just thinking. Did you say which one I could change? Choose. I'd choose . . . I don't see why school children always have to wear school uniform. I don't like wearing school uniform. I'd like to wear just something more comfortable or something that you want to wear. Like we're just sort of forced to be wearing a uniform just because we're going to that school and we have to let people know what school we're going to. I think we should be free to do what we want.

Rozita has a masterful grasp of the communicative function of language. Although at times she makes an imprecise use of grammar (and these uses are different in kind from the errors we all make in speech) her communication of meaning is never affected. She uses language in several functions, even in this fairly formal questionnaire situation; there is no doubt that she is well-equipped in her English to control her own affairs within her new culture. What is missing, though, from Rozita's transcript is a demonstration of the analytic competence that Fiona reveals. It is clear that Rozita's schooling has given her the skill to know when to speak, what about, and at what level of explicitness; but in the latter questions (4 and 5), which demand a use of the explanatory function of language, there is not much evidence in her responses of her subordinating reality to possibility by making judgements and by creating new hypotheses. Instead there are many unargued assertions ("you don't kill them", "you can sort it out like humans", "I don't like wearing school uniform") which are adequate replies but which suggest that Rozita has not yet emerged into that stage of "intoxication with logic" that Fiona has reached. At the same time, from her detailed reply to question 3, we can assume that she is not far away from displaying analytic competence in her oral language. Moreover, having seen written work from Rozita I can say that she reveals a higher level of analytic competence in that language mode. In order to prompt her into reproducing that competence in her spoken language, Rozita might benefit greatly from rich discussions with her peers, especially if there were a good mixture of competencies in those discussion participants.

Romeo is a fifteen year old whose first language is Italian:

1. *Would you tell me all about that last school of yours?*

Well, I found that that school was very enjoyable and it, like in common with my friends I learnt a lot and enjoyed going to school there. I found the teachers very co-operative and good friends and they helped me a lot. The classrooms, they were usually very decorative and they were large to a degree, you know; many people were in the classrooms, about thirty in each class. And there was lots of art-work and things that the class participated in were hung, pinned up around the classroom. Oh, from the outside it, it looked fairly old 'cause it was built I think in 1917. But it has withstood the weathering and things like that very well. It looked very neat I think.

2. *What did you like about that school?*
. . . I just liked the people at the school. The teachers were very friendly and didn't insult you and things like that. They gave me a good sense of security really.

3. *Would you say it was a good school? Why?*
Yes I would. Oh just the fact that there was a lot of grass and a lot of playing areas for the kids and . . . I disliked the fact that the steelworks were right next door but you can't help that.

4. *Would you say that telling a lie is always wrong?*
Oh in certain, certain circumstances a little white lie doesn't go astray because you maybe don't want to hurt a person's feelings or something and so you tell them a, a lie just to, you know, not to make them feel bad.

5. *Would you lie to save a friend's life?*
Yes, I would. Oh yeah, it might be sort of futuristic whatever, but if a dictatorship or militaristic sort of outlook came upon Australia and people were going around collecting friends of mine because of the religion or race that they came from and if they asked me if they were of a particular race, I would say that they weren't from the race they were collecting prisoners for or whatever.

6. *Would you say that killing another person is always wrong?*
Oh I think killing is, no-one's got the right to kill someone else because God gave you life and only He can take it away. But in a case like euthanasia, well a, a close person or something who's, who's dying slowly and suffering a lot, you know, you wouldn't want to be put through that hardship so you might, it might sound strange, but you might put the person out of their misery by killing them, painlessly and quickly.

Romeo displays a rather formal use of language that is not uncommon among adolescents whose mother tongue is not English: the "courtesies" of language use (as taught in formal ESL classes) are observed by making things as explicit as possible; by attending in his answers to the point of the questions. He uses his language to express considerable insight into human behaviour and human problems. For example, in 6 he reasons in terms of a moral law ("because God gave you life") and speculates about the exception to that law that euthanasia suggests, thereby tapping into an over-riding ethical principle that is for him on a higher level than a moral law; this is a sophisticated example of analytic competence at work. Like Fiona, he introduces concepts that reflect his encounters with abstract notions: "euthanasia", "weathering", "futuristic", "dictatorship", "militaristic". Also like Fiona, his use of difficult concepts is accompanied by a use of conditional structures and hypothetical settings for his discourse: in 2, "they gave me a good sense of security really"; in 4, "in certain circumstances maybe you don't want to hurt a person's feelings", in 6, "you might put a person out of their misery"; and in 5, Romeo constructs an involved and colourful setting for staging the resolution of his hypothetical case. He has a mastery of English that is undeniable and well in tune with the demands of his own society.

There are many factors in their development that have influenced the quality and richness of the oral (and written) language of these two immigrant children. These might include: parental pressure to succeed in schooling, common among immigrant families in tightly-knit communities and observed in the community under study; their employment as translators, from their earliest years, by monolingual relatives, thereby meeting topics for translation in the new culture that were oriented to adult and real-world experiences; and the transfer benefits that a strong grasp of a first language can bring to the learning and use of a second. For this discussion, though, the relevant factor to be recognized is the rich oral-language-based atmosphere that was provided in their schooling. Throughout their education they encountered oral language across the curriculum.

Peel & de Silva's conclusions (1972) about adolescent conceptual learning have already been mentioned several times: before the age of fifteen it is difficult for children to acquire the meanings of difficult words passively from their contexts, whether those contexts are literary or verbal. If new words are first encountered only through a piece of prose or through the utterances of a teacher, it is likely that their meanings will not be grasped; the words will not be available for later use in thought or language.

Fiona's proficiency in word use may be due in large part to her coming from a family background where high priority has been placed on the use of language to share meanings; she has probably had rich and experience-based encounters with words and been encouraged to use them in a motivated way. These are only speculations on my part, although they are based on a close familiarity with Fiona's school and her classmates; it is certain that she has had no long-term special attention in her school that is any different from that received by her classmates.

Yet Fiona, and others drawn from relatively privileged middle class backgrounds, far exceed in their lexical proficiency their classmates drawn from low-income backgrounds, even while matched in school experience and in non-verbal reasoning ability. In the case of Rozita and Romeo, however, similar conclusions cannot be drawn; both of these adolescents came from *low-income* and non-English speaking family backgrounds, backgrounds at the beginning of their school careers which did not augur well for English language development. For these children, though, the school compensated for what the home could not provide. It is possible that fifteen-year-olds from low-income families, who may have narrow life experiences when compared with their privileged peers, will not have developed their lexical range to the same degree. It is likely, on the evidence, that they will have remained very much at the same level as twelve-year-olds, unless the school has done something about it.

In Fiona's case, as mentioned, the school was not offering any particular programme aimed at improving language skills, any programme that was specifically targeted on those without a rich language background (nor would any programme of this type be of much value, since each child's language needs are so individual as to make the design of an effective compensatory programme an impossibility). In explaining Fiona's language proficiency, and the proficiency of others like her, teachers have often concluded wrongly that these children are simply more intelligent and that this explains their proficiency. Yet all the children used in the studies I am reporting here were matched for non-verbal reasoning ability. Equality in intelligence on its own, though, does not guarantee equality in intellectual development, if the material resource for that development is not present somewhere in the environment of the child. If the school does not provide that material resource then some children will miss out. The need in providing that material resource at the senior secondary level, as in earlier stages of schooling, is for *experience-based* conceptual development.

Experience-based work meets new difficulties in the senior school. Most of the words to be acquired are abstract in meaning. How can the meanings of abstract words be "experienced" if those meanings exist only in the minds of language users and not in concrete reality? The answer to this seems to lie in the intellectual demands presented by *discourse*. Dialogue and discussion, on subject matter using the terminology and the meanings to be learned, help the acquisition of complex ideas. Carefully organized and directed discourse can ask children to use new terms and relate them to other known terms. Meaning is clarified in the act of trying out new words in our own speech and hearing them used in reply in the original speech of others. Without this experience of word use, new words encountered may remain dormant forever in our passive vocabulary. Oral language work provides the principal method for achieving this objective.

The teaching of words

Across the senior school curriculum there is an important place for the teaching of words: words that name new ideas, and the relationships necessary for manipulating those ideas in thought and language. Very often in schools *word teaching* and *word learning* become distinct activities: students are not "learning words" even though teachers believe that they are "teaching" them. Effective education in "words" involves introducing terms to serve a natural function in the teaching and learning process, not teaching them as "syllabus items" to be acquired at any cost. In Britton's view (1970) it is from successive experience of words in use — words used for some actual profit or pleasure — that children build up their resources; he believes that there is little point in our dragging things in by their names. The *links* between the meanings of words provide strong clues to their meanings. For these clues to be gleaned words need to be used in contexts that carry meaning for the word learner. The best example of a context for word learning by adolescent children is one that invites their own utterances, employing words in serious dialogue with other children or the teacher.

Barnes (1976) mentions a "language of secondary education" which he subdivides into two categories: the *sociocultural* and the *conceptual*. Teachers are obliged to use new words from the conceptual category to express important meanings relevant to their subjects. Words from Barnes' sociocultural category, however, relate more to the speaker's attitude to his or her present role. They are mildly pretentious words, used to create an aura of expertise while conveying meanings which can be expressed alternatively in an effective yet less pretentious way. For example, in an early draft of this chapter I used the word "interdependencies" where the word "links" now appears in the previous paragraph. There may be occasions where "interdependencies" lends greater precision to the meaning to be expressed, but that paragraph was not one of them; and "links" seems as effective. In introducing terminology teachers need to be clear that their use of novel words is controlled by the needs of the subject and not by a vain attempt to present children with some high-status jargon of the school, a jargon, which some will learn to mimic but which others will learn to despise and avoid in their everyday communication.

Timing the introduction of specialist words is as important a consideration as finding methods for getting them into the mouths of students (Marland, 1977). At one extreme words can be inefficiently presented in a formal vocabulary session, perhaps months before the meanings of the words are encountered. At the other extreme words can be hastily presented by the teacher in the middle of an activity, with no recourse to meaning analysis and no opportunity for students to put the meaning into use. The recommended approach is to introduce the word as near as possible to the experience or subject matter to which it relates. Immediate attention can then be given to its use by students, promoting that use through one or more of the approaches to oral language work available as methodologies across the senior school curriculum.

Approaches to oral language work

Discussion as a part of whole class teaching

Whole class discussion can be a rather futile venture at any stage of schooling. The realities of large classes and lack of student knowledge block the creation of real dialogue between teacher and pupils. Very often the "discussion" becomes a monologue or at best a dialogue with one or two star pupils. By the senior school there is more chance of benefits accruing from whole class discussion, even with fairly large classes. Success depends upon the presentation of stimulating subject matter and especially upon the personal attributes of the teacher (see below). While preserving for themselves the right to direct and to channel the talk, strong teachers can afford to make suggestions that the children are free to reject. This "freedom to reject" depends on the teacher approaching discussion in a way which makes it clear to the children that there is a difference between suggestion and instruction. This approach also insists that teachers share the talking time. A hard lesson for teachers to learn is to be silent.

Grambs & Carr (1979) suggest the following strategy when a provocative issue has been posed: say nothing at first; look around the room expectantly, waiting and watching for an inevitable response. They advise that in leading discussion, teachers direct their statements at non-contributors; that they "demand knowledge" from the children; and that they weave the children's interests and skills into the discussion. They propose *five personal attributes* that the good discussion leader should have: a personal and lively interest in the subject of the discussion; an open mind about the outcomes or the pattern of discussion; a sense of the humorous as well as of the serious; a genuine interest in the opinions of young people; and an ability to suppress their own opinions most of the time. Self (1976) presents ways of cultivating the desire to talk and also provides his own "attributes that a discussion leader should possess".

Barnes (in Marland, 1977:174) frames questions that teachers could ask themselves about their approach to whole class discussion; he admits that these reflect his own bias about what makes "good teaching". His seven questions deserve quoting in full:

1. Are you requiring your pupils to think for themselves or mainly asking them to feed back information from a book or from an earlier lesson?
2. Are you eliciting the pupils' existing experience and understanding and working from that, or does the way you are planning lessons tend to make their present knowledge irrelevant?
3. Do your responses to pupils' contributions include replies which use and develop what they have said, or are you predominantly evaluating replies as right/wrong, or good/bad?
4. When you present information, or give a demonstration, or read a poem, or discuss a visit, are you requiring your pupils to explain and hypothesize, or are you telling them what it means?
5. Do you ask pupils to expand what they have said, to respond to one another, to ask questions, to offer evidence, to consider alternative explanations, to plan lines of action?
6. Are your pupils in fact contributing at some length to the lessons, or answering merely in brief phrases?
7. Are they raising questions of their own, offering experiences and opinions, joining in the formulating of knowledge?

The approach that the teacher adopts to "*questioning*" is an important variable in whole class discussion; I raise it here only in a cautionary way. It is a mistake to believe that there is any role in genuine whole class discussion for the kinds of questions that teachers very often need to use in the more didactic side of their work. The questions asked in classrooms are often more akin to what happens in doctors' surgeries or in courtrooms (Wardhaugh, 1985; Edwards & Furlong, 1978); they are more often challenges or investigatory charges than invitations to engage in discourse.

It is important that teachers know the effects of these differences: their impact upon the attitudes and sensitivities of young people; and their implications for the learning process. Barnes (in Barnes, Britton & Torbe, 1986) examines the types of questions that teachers are likely to ask in classrooms; he finds a predominance of factual over reasoning questions; he points to the near absence of genuinely open questions, questions calling for neither reasoning nor any particular answer: the sort of questions that we use to invite dialogue. Later he suggests that there are implications for control and classroom management in the kinds of questions that teachers ask. Some teachers may be trapped into a "restrictive pedagogy" based on the use of closed questions by their fears of losing control of pupils. For many, though, the habit may be nothing more than an ingrained way of doing things that deserves changing. Sometimes I have noticed a "teachers' disease": teachers become so used to their role as inquisitors that they are unable to step outside it, even when they prefer to promote learning through a conversational approach. A book like Wardhaugh's *How Conversation Works* could be a useful reference for those at risk.

Where whole class work is essential (and it often is) there are good reasons for using small group work as a preparation for the large group discussion. Meanings, opinions and positions can be "thought out loud" in the security of a small group; small groups provide an opportunity to rehearse the later public performance of points and positions; and an atmosphere of worthwhileness is created for whole class discussion when the teacher values the process of discussion itself enough to ensure a preliminary exchange of opinions on the topic.

Group discussion

This approach receives major attention here since its importance as a pedagogy in learning grows the older children become. At this stage of schooling teachers are concerned to encourage children to *discover their own meanings*. Indeed, the way that the process of learning proceeds suggests that this is very nearly the only way at this level for teaching to be approached. Children by late adolescence bring such vast differences in experience, knowledge, values and attitudes to the classroom that it is impossible for us as teachers to respond to their conjectures or theories about the world in a uniform way; their major "theories" are all so different, and filled with error in such unique ways, that children must be brought to take the responsibility themselves for testing out their own conjectures and reformulating them on the basis of evidence encountered.

Speech plays the main part in this complex process. The more that learners control their own language use, thinking aloud and responding to others thinking aloud, the more they can be responsible for formulating explanatory hypotheses and evaluating them. Discussion may be of little use in learning catalogues of factual knowledge. Its value lies in helping students to grasp principles and to use the new knowledge to recode old knowledge and experience. In this process of relating new knowledge to old (often in ways which the teacher overlooks or cannot imagine: Barnes, 1976) adolescents establish the meanings of new concepts for themselves; they learn how concepts are linked in meaning; and they eliminate error from their theories about the world. The learning of the new provokes a re-use of the old in language; a wide active use of words, usually only passively held, is promoted.

By the senior school most children have worked out for themselves a few rules for "good conversation" even if they have never been asked to state them. They realize, too, that discussion, like good conversation, needs support of a practical kind from participants if it is going to be effective. The following list of "rules for conversation and discussion" was prepared by group members in study and discussion programmes that I have organized:

1. share the talking time: if there are five people in a discussion, aim to talk about one-fifth of the time;
2. pat-the-ball-back: when your contribution has been made, hand discussion over to another, by question or gesture;
3. make contributions brief, limiting them if possible to a few sentences;
4. marshall all your listening and concentration powers when others are talking;
5. follow the train of the discussion and try to develop it with your contributions, not destroy it;
6. speak confidently and carefully in the knowledge that you have the full attention of other group members;
7. avoid boasting, name dropping or point-scoring;
8. give attention and respect to the other side of the issue.

Point 8 can be the most worthwhile and difficult to follow of these "rules". Britton (in Barnes, Britton & Torbe, 1986) mentions "Rogerian debate", suggesting how the members of very small groups can pay deliberate attention to the viewpoints of one another: A tries on B's viewpoint and sees how the world looks from that angle; B is there to assist and "check the position" as it develops; when B is satisfied that the view has been properly formulated by A, B listens while A tries to say what there is in common between the two points of view.

The "rules" above provide only rough guidelines that are certainly worthy of discussion themselves. One school, the Abraham Moss Centre in Manchester, takes pupil discussion very seriously: they have developed techniques for "discussing discussion". A worksheet of some of the approaches used in this school is presented in Marland (1977).

Making effective conversationalists out of young people is not widely accepted as one of the senior school's central roles (Adler, 1983), although views on this matter are changing as "education for work" becomes a more central concern of those schools operating in contexts of chronic unemployment for young people. Young adults who cannot present themselves effectively in conversation may not be welcomed by prospective employers, if the employers have a range of applicants to choose from and need some criterion for excluding candidates. The development of conversational competence is a serious part of senior school teaching, then, that is little addressed, perhaps because no sector of the curriculum sees it as a direct concern. There are simple principles governing turn-taking in conversations, for example, that can be communicated readily to children and practised as well when discussion techniques are a regular courtesy of the classroom. Wardhaugh (1985) suggests the following principles:

1. one and only one person speaks at a time.
2. the end of an item of conversation is signalled by a change of pitch or pace; by pausing; or by a gesture of relaxation.
3. an interest in speaking in the conversation is signalled by bodily movements or an intake of breath.
4. interruptions depend on a successful application of strategies, if they are not to be resisted by speakers.
5. closing a conversation is a co-operative activity.

Getting the right "mix" of students in adolescent discussion is vital to its success. Even self-selected friendship groups may not guarantee good results for all groups. Careful use of a questionnaire gives basic information, which can be more detailed perhaps than the questionnaire mentioned in Chapter 4. In this instance pupils can be asked to nominate their two closest friends *and* perhaps one person not liked as well; perhaps, too, teachers can state the purpose of the questionnaire quite openly: "a work group"; "a team mate"; "a travelling companion", etc. (Grambs & Carr, 1979). Teachers can quickly filter the results of this questionnaire through their own knowledge of the children in order to create groups of mixed ability and some harmony. Even so, there will be difficulties for some groups. Here the great advantage of small group work surfaces for teachers as they are freed to give full attention to groups or individuals who have these difficulties. There is a balance required, though, in this teacher involvement, between avoiding a teacher domination that discourages pupils from active learning and at the other extreme abandoning pupils to their own devices.

The object of group discussion in schooling is to *promote learning.* This aim of the activity needs to be made clear to adolescents, especially where group work is novel for them. Group work can be introduced to senior students unfamiliar with it by creating small committees to assist in administering classrooms (the bulletin board, the chemistry lab., the distribution of materials) or by using "buzz groups" to canvas opinion on issues and directions, in a minimum of time with maximum participation (Grambs & Carr, 1979). A buzz group is useful for small group activities that take up only a portion of a class period. Its membership dissolves as soon as the group talk is ended. An extension of this approach is the "fish bowl method" which proceeds in three stages: 1) small groups meet for five minutes discussion on an issue; 2) each group instructs its representative on its position on the issue and relevant points; 3) all the representatives debate the issue publicly in the centre of the class, with or without communication by group members with their representatives.

Chilver & Gould (1982) offer a transcript of five sixteen-year-olds engaged in group discussion. The children's task is to plan a history essay on a given topic, having previously worked on that topic in class. They have a reference text with them and they have worked together in groups before. There are several features of the discussion, as recorded, that are characteristic of group work at this level: a leader emerges quickly, who formulates a strategy of operation and who uses his own greater insights into the particular topic as a basis for his influence; points made by others and their points-of-view are accepted as valid contributions; the taking-of-turns follows a liberal and democratic pattern; and there is no attempt to win points. At the same time, perhaps because of too great an emphasis on consideration and courtesy, opportunities for exploring issues in depth are missed; this is a real risk when the "courtesies" are overstressed. Barnes & Todd (1977) analyse these issues in detail. In good discussion work disagreements lead to attempted conflict resolution, and from this learning proceeds: children's conjectures about the world are changed; error is eliminated from their theories.

The following exchanges took place among a group of three fifteen-year-old Australian children from a mixed ability class. They had already had an extended history of moving into discussion groups at various times during the school day. On this occasion the children's task was to answer several questions after reading a passage and looking at some related pictures; their answers were to be noted and reported back to the whole class:

Paul: "Read the passage titled 'Savonarola and Florence' . . ."
Susan: Let's do that, then . . .

Paul: Finished? . . . Will you read the first question, Damien?
Damien: Right . . . "How did one man, and a friar at that, come to be so influential in Florence when that city was already at the peak of its power?" . . . OK?
Susan: Yes, I've been thinking about the first question while we've been reading . . . well, the answer to that is . . . the answer's really . . . it's contained in the passage, isn't it?
Paul: No . . . no, it only says that the people of Florence . . . "the Florentines were very religious but were unhappy with the way the Church was governed at that time" . . . we need more than that, don't we?
Susan: Yes, but it goes on to say things about Sav . . . Sav-on-a-rola . . . I find that hard to say . . .
Damien: Sounds a bit like "saveloy" . . . "battered sav"! (laughs)
Susan: . . . that he was . . . how impressive he was as a person. Look what it says . . . "seemed to have the gift of prophecy. He had foretold the deaths of the Pope and Lorenzo the Magnificent . . ."
Damien: . . . and "a very impressive speaker in the Church" . . . yeah . . .
Paul: Well, does this mean he had what they wanted . . . sort of . . . as a leader, or what?
Damien: We could write . . .
Susan: Yes, he had the people's support . . . because of his personality, sort of a thing . . . but . . . but isn't there more to it . . .?
Damien: Wait a minute, I want to get this down . . .

Damien: I'll read the last question, all right? . . . "Look at the painting 'A fiery death is provided for Savonarola outside the town hall in Florence' . . . What can you say about Savonarola's supporters from this painting?" . . .
Susan: Well . . . some of them are going to be burned too . . . are

already burning with him . . .

Paul: Yeah, but what about those others? . . . They're friars like Sav. was . . .

Susan: They're frightened . . . looking away . . .

Damien: I'm not surprised, it's horrible!

Susan: . . . yes but they're not . . .

Paul: yes . . . they are frightened, but it's not the burning . . . it's . . . it's fear of . . . you know . . . getting caught . . .

Susan: They don't want to be "identified by the authorities", isn't that it? . . .

Damien: I'm not surprised at that, either.

Paul: Are these an answer, then?

Several features stand out in this impressive piece of communal learning; the children are obviously relaxed with the activity and with one another; they give and take directions without rancour; they are able to risk disagreement, in fact they seem to thrive on it; they pass the discussion around, supporting one another's comments even while disagreeing. It is fairly clear that one child, Susan, has a superior grasp of the subject matter and its language, yet she does not impose this on the others. Another child, Paul, seems to be aware of Susan's strength and stimulates it with his tentative contributions, looking for clarification and an extension of his own ideas. The third child, Damien, sees his role (and is seen) as co-ordinator of things; he is also an occasional contributor and a facilitator, using humour on one occasion to edge the process along. There is much more that could be said about this exemplary piece of discourse. The most important thing, though, is to highlight the individual learning that proceeds: each child, in very different ways, speculates, offers tentative conjectures and eliminates error from those conjectures. Knowledge and understanding are growing.

Role play

The unprepared, unrehearsed dramatization used in role play is well suited to the interests and temperaments of senior school children. Drawing on material from any source, role play can be a telling device in its impact, providing an unforgettable experience for individuals attempting to think themselves into roles which are not their own. Britton (1970) provides a transcript of adolescent role playing in which participants go some way towards making other people's problems their own temporarily. He concludes that the children are forced to recognize aspects of a situation that they might otherwise ignore, making any subsequent discussion to that extent less blinkered and more inclusive.

There are six recommended steps in employing the approach (Grambs & Carr, 1979): 1) select the role play situation; 2) choose the participants; 3) create the setting, through discussion in small groups of role players; 4) prepare the audience, by inviting them to ask themselves "is this the way *you* act and feel" and by urging them to get inside the characters; 5) act out the situation, looking for no finished product but stressing the exploratory nature of the exercise; and 6) invite a follow-up comment from the audience and from the role players themselves who report how they felt. The exercise can be repeated with new characters or some thematic variation. Role play is useful for getting the first draft of a script for radio, for video-work or for plays. Expressive writing, removed from the humdrum artificiality of much school written work, can follow from an effective role playing exercise. More important still, in sophisticated role play situations there is a fine integration of activities that are relevant to both *communicative and analytic competence*. While being asked to assume the role of another by demonstrating the presumed communicative responses of that other, students are forced to undertake a double cognitive task: thinking about the social role of that other, and using language to project the interpretation of the role that they are thinking about.

Simulation games are a combination of role play and improvisation activities. These are explored by Self (1976) and Grambs & Carr (1979). Mills (1977) suggests ways in which teachers can design their own simulation games for use with mixed ability groups; in an Appendix he lists materials and sources for games and simulations in the senior school. Stringer (1977) confirms the value of simulation games for upper secondary groups: they give insights into social problems, such as the difficulties of tenement families, which cannot easily be brought into the classroom in any other way. A BBC booklet (Longley, 1972) contains details of suitable activities; however, since simulation games in schools are booming, it would be useful to look through issues of educational journals and magazines in your field, particularly looking at advertisements, to pick up the most recent games and simulation activities that are commercially available.

Pair work

This is a variation on small group work, which suits the close relationships developed in adolescence. In the intimate setting of one-to-one work, children are more likely to allow their "inner dialogue" to be released, questioning and re-appraising their own ideas and statements in the company of a well-known companion. It is here where the application of "Rogerian debate" comes into its own (see above, pages 105–6, and

Britton, in Barnes, Britton & Torbe, 1986). A Schools Council Working Paper (1979) records in transcript an example of effective pair work in an English Literature class: two senior school girls answer questions allotted to them, using a method of their own devising; one girl reads the question and establishes her own tentative solution, setting it against the evidence and against her own ideas; the other girl questions this solution until she can see points of agreement. Evolving from this is a statement amalgamating both points of view in a way which satisfies both girls. They proceed through the questions, reversing roles alternately and devising for themselves a very successful strategy.

Discussion and communication in pair work can be encouraged in any subject by using "cloze" passages, relevant to classwork. The operation involved in finding the right words to fill blanks in passages drawn from textbooks is a great stimulus to oral language use; there is a concentration on shades of meaning, getting it right and sharing knowledge. As in all small group work, practice increases both the sophistication and the efficiency of the strategies and the methods children devise; a sharpening of their critical faculties follows. This development and awareness of their critical powers is a key advance for older children to make; it is an essential attribute if their own knowledge is to grow.

The debate

Self (1976) warns against the use of the formal debate on the grounds that it can ensure the minimum of talk from the minimum number of participants. Certainly oral spontaneity disappears within the disciplined framework of a formal debate. It is an activity for the upper years of the senior school; it has value in encouraging speakers to appreciate other points of view and to do some preliminary work in order to make themselves relatively expert in the subject matter. However, it is a use of language usually serving one function only: the performative "task" of persuasion. Harvey (1968) and Burniston (1968) have much to say about the role and the evaluation of debates. The emphasis in both these authors, however, is upon the "assessment" of oral language performance and these assessment procedures become the "curriculum of oral language"; their bias, then, is away from oral language as a tool for learning, which is my stress in this book.

Public speaking

This is also an activity best reserved for the upper years of the senior school. Self (1976) gives an extensive treatment of what he calls "talking in public". In presenting their own skills, discoveries and interests, by using apparatus, pictures and diagrams, adolescents gain some confidence in their talk by becoming an authority for a time. Motivation arises from the pleasure of communicating specialist knowledge to an audience. However, the effect on the audience, and the feedback to the speaker, can be deadening if the talk is written and rehearsed beforehand. By asking speakers to deal with particular questions or issues, rather than with topics or subjects, teachers can discourage speakers from dull and descriptive presentations; a lively dialogue may follow as well. Lively, natural and spontaneous English is more likely to be promoted through providing unscripted answers to other students' questions, after the preliminary talk. It is in this process, too, with the teacher joining in, that real learning by students can be elicited and follow-up work devised. Again Harvey (1968) and Burniston (1968) provide a good deal of practical information, which is perhaps now rather out of touch with contemporary views and theories (see previous section). Marland (1977) sees public speaking as virtually a separate concern whose methods have little to offer in the encouragement of communicative talk in a school. I agree with this view.

Across the senior school curriculum

This section should be read in close conjunction with its sister section in Chapter 4. The division of the senior school curriculum below attempts to follow in a logical way philosophical discussion on what forms of knowledge might be represented in the secondary school curriculum. I attempt to conform once again to the "forms of knowledge and experience" that were first introduced in Chapter 4. My caveat mentioned in that context (page 79) about the limitations of curricular mapping systems applies here once again.

Discussion falls under five sub-headings: 1) the humanities (social studies/human sciences); 2) the physical sciences; 3) mathematics; 4) expressive arts, creative arts and human movement; and 5) values education.

The Humanities (Social Studies/Human Sciences)

Whole class discussion and group discussion are key approaches available to the Humanities teacher in the senior school. An early attempt at an integrated programme, the Humanities Curriculum Project in Britain, (HCP), used a single blend of whole class and small group discussion as its principal methodology (Macdonald & Walker, 1976). The

HCP remains a fruitful source of insights, both theoretical and practical. It is easy to place the HCP in the category of "values education" as well, since it is concerned with adolescent pupils discussing controversial social *and* moral issues. The stated aim of the HCP was "to develop an understanding of human acts, of social situations, and of the problems of value which arise from them". The question for schools it posed was "how is a teacher in a democracy to handle controversial issues?" Five premises were accepted in answering this question:

1. controversial issues *should* be handled in the classroom with adolescents;
2. teachers should adopt a stance of "neutrality", regarding it as part of their responsibility not to promote their own views;
3. discussion, not instruction, is the teaching approach suited to the aim;
4. divergence of views, rather than consensus, should be encouraged;
5. teachers as discussion chairpersons should be responsible for quality and standards in learning.

The HCP covered nine themes, offering collections of study materials and teachers' guides. These were to be used in classroom discussion with the teachers attempting to promote reflection and an interpretation of the evidence drawn from the theme collections. Mixed ability groups of no more than 15 students, using circular seating arrangements in a semi-formal atmosphere, were recommended.

The debate that followed the introduction of the HCP sets into a real world context a central issue in using oral language at the senior level. Opponents of the approach used in the HCP argued that pupils must be able to understand the material *before* they can discuss it. Advocates of the HCP claimed that understanding is the *product* not the *prerequisite* of discussion: talk can promote understanding; it does not depend upon it. The HCP, along with other curriculum kits such as the SEMP project in Australia (Social Education Materials Project) represent early attempts to design programmes in Humanities which had discussion work as their central approach. While the material content of both of these programmes is now out-of-date, the controversies they produced and the methods they recommended continue to provide subject matter for teacher discussion on the use of oral learning situations in the Humanities.

Teachers of individual school subjects that are cross-disciplinary, but which have a considerable "human sciences" content, can use oral methods to *integrate* the various areas of knowledge and experience that these subjects include. The approach that I am suggesting here has already been described at length in Chapter 4. In Ancient Civilizations, for example, a group discussion can be mounted preliminary to a piece of individual writing; this discussion might consider some issue whose possible solutions will draw on a variety of perspectives. For instance, the task of deciding "the importance and meaning of the Parthenon for fifth century Athenians", using pictorial sources showing scenes from the temple's friezes and metopes, might integrate discussion on any of the following: the imperial history of Periclean Athens; the geography of the Athenian Empire; the legends represented on the friezes themselves; the religious symbolism of the building and its surroundings; and the art and architecture of the period.

English Literature, too, is a humanities area where group discussion can be used by children to bring their own views and understandings to share with one another. Literature provides rich subject matter for confronting values issues and learning moral concepts: a discussion addressing a single chapter of one of Thomas Hardy's novels, for example, could lead to a rich appreciation of the use of some of our culture's moral concepts, such as "indignation", "benevolence" or "condolence". This task of learning moral concepts and confronting values issues is often best undertaken away from the real concerns of students themselves, in a context of impersonality and objectivity. Borrowing moral dilemmas that are faced by the protagonists in quality literature can provide material for debates, role play, improvisation, pair work and group work.

Grambs & Carr (1979) suggest discussion group approaches for use in home economics classes and in business economics classes. In the former the teacher assigns students (presumably boys and girls) to "kitchens" made up of four students each, who each have the job of solving as a group the problems that relate to the units of instruction (e.g. producing a series of balanced meals, using nutrition guidelines); in the business economics class, groups are set up according to the divisions of a large office and work through a problem in office management.

In approaching social issues, looking at "homes and families" in an integrated Humanities programme, the simulation game is a valuable way of lending vicarious experience to complex problems. Introducing the game "*Tenement*", for example, (Stringer, 1977) group discussion work precedes the simulation, with information injected using worksheets that describe characters, the conditions of buildings, and the attributes of seven families who live in the tenement block; the "simulation" itself calls for the playing out of the roles of these seven families by seven small groups of students. Follow-up work is suggested, again using a rich blend of oral language activities and ending in purposeful writing exercises. In similar vein, interviews are useful role play exercises in which children playing the role of journalists or social workers put questions to role players operating in controversial social circumstances. Self (1976) discusses the interview and its value in vocational preparation. A Schools Council paper (1979) presents examples of the interview technique used in real classes.

The physical sciences

Science tries to provide tentative theories, in response to problem situations, and to eliminate error from those theories. At every stage in this process dialogue informs progress: identifying the problem, formulating the tentative theory, subjecting it to critical test statements and formulating a new theory. Knowledge in the sciences grows from the use of criticism: a thought once formulated in language becomes an object outside ourselves that is available for criticism; it becomes a theory about the world which itself is susceptible to error elimination. Tentative theories, of the kind proposed by serious senior students in the sciences, can be stated and examined in no more rigorous a way than through dialogue: small group discussion work is essential to the learning process in the sciences. More than this, very often students do not know *what* their tentative theories are until they have had to state them.

A study of the history of science, and a study of the development of the various themes and branches in science that have become disciplines, is an essential element in a science curriculum. The history of science is a rich source of topics for improvisation activities through which students can be brought to view the development of science as a gradual process of eliminating error from our tentative theories. Examples abound in the lives of Medieval and Renaissance scientists: Galileo, Da Vinci, Copernicus and Tycho Brah; or in the stories handed down about ancient thinkers like Archimedes and Pythagoras. The task in learning is to see how these people overturned the prejudices and the beliefs of their time and in so doing advanced our knowledge about the cosmos. Teachers can begin improvisation work, for example, by asking children to create a scene that depicts the "closed-mindedness" that preceded the discovery in question; from this beginning children in their drama work can construct the chain of events that overturned the false dogma, capturing some of the mental and physical anguish perhaps that accompanied the iconoclasm.

Senior adolescents can take much of the responsibility for learning the new concepts that they need in their disciplines, since they are able to work out meanings quite readily from the context of textbooks. This conceptual learning can be heightened by a deliberate and regular use of pair work on cloze passages drawn from difficult texts. In a cloze reading assignment, pairs or small groups of children are given a passage from which every ninth or tenth word has been deleted. The point of the exercise is to close the gaps appropriately with a single word in each case; the activity promotes rich discussion: learning proceeds.

Six stages in a science teacher's "circus method" for sixteen-year-olds are presented in a Schools Council Working Paper (1979). Beginning with a lesson mainly of *teacher talk,* the sequence proceeds through stages of *small group work* in measurement, reading and discussion; *whole class discussion* in which results and problems are explained; a further stage of *small group work* in which everyone becomes fully involved with the idea of the topic; a further *whole class discussion* devoted to an oral consideration of the original goal; and a *final stage* in which groups extend and predict from the findings of the earlier work. While stressing the value of talk in this approach, the teacher does not let pupils talk for the sake of talking. He carefully structures talk into a whole learning programme so that pupils talk in a variety of circumstances and to a variety of purposes.

Self (1976) suggests how public speaking by pupils can be used effectively for communicating "hard" knowledge in science. Robertson (in Marland, 1977) offers a detailed study of how talking and learning combine in science. She describes a sequence of lessons in physics with mixed ability fourth year boys. This sequence suggests how science can be approached by students tackling problems in a context where critical talk is set firmly within the problem situation.

Mathematics

Perhaps nowhere else in the curriculum is oral work used less than in senior school Maths, yet some approach to learning in which Maths concepts are used in a motivated way in children's dialogue does seem essential for promoting mathematical conceptual understanding (see points on this subject in Chapter 4). A Schools Council Working Paper (1979) in three case studies shows how small group discussion work may be incorporated as an approach in the Maths lesson; a novel approach in "learning to ask the right question" in Maths, through a process of "reflexivity" in discussion, is explained and evaluated.

A combination of work cards and pair work, using students with similar mathematical strengths, can promote an appreciation of the logic of problem-solving in Maths. People more readily locate errors in the course of a computation if they are asked to explain to another the ways in which errors could have occurred. Very often teachers themselves lack the time to engage in this form of dialogue with every child: peer learning in pair work is a fruitful and efficient alternative. On the other hand even public speaking is a possibility in senior Maths, as Self (1976) shows in listing possible activities.

Expressive arts, creative arts and human movement

The lengthy discussion on this topic in Chapter 4 is relevant here, too. By the senior school individual work in the visual arts is the norm. Yet the role of criticism grows in importance the more our creations become idiosyncratic ones: language is the only objective standard of assessment that is available to us in the arts; its use for this purpose can only be acquired in complex exchanges of interpretation, centred on the objects of creation themselves. In this way the subjective views of a number of people can come together and establish, in language, objective norms upon which there is some measure of agreement. It is so easy to talk nonsense in the creative arts: the boundary between sense and nonsense is a fine one, yet it is not an absolute one either. A useful grasp of the language of assessment and criticism in the arts will most profitably come from engaging in talk with those who themselves have thought deeply about standards in creative endeavours and discussed those standards with people who themselves are concerned to develop creative excellence. What all this suggests is that whole class, small group or individual discussion, centred upon the teacher or some guest in the role of the expert, is central to heightening children's appreciation of their own work and the work of others. Discussion groups using critical texts which themselves become topics for criticism are a supplementary approach. In all this, though, the role of the teacher, as the experienced interlocutor equipped with the language of criticism, is the central one.

In the performing arts senior students are ready to work co-operatively in groups towards a goal decided by the group. Group music-making, for example, in which small improvised compositions are planned and rehearsed, demands co-operative talk. The musical products are offered, doubted, assessed and decided (Marland, 1977). Children's individual and choral singing can be made more meaningful and expressive if the song lyrics are discussed for their sense and purpose in advance. A Schools Council paper (1979) discusses and gives examples of talk applied in and across music activities. Perhaps the chief place for oral work in the performing arts is when students are encouraged to evaluate each other's work through discussion: through critical dialogue students learn that each one's aesthetic experience is different, while still remaining valid for the individual.

In games, small group discussion finds a ready-made structure in the need to plan team tactics and strategies: netball and basketball teams provide discussion groups of an ideal size; the backs and forwards of various football teams, and the bowlers, pitchers, batters and batsmen from cricket and baseball teams, suggest groups that can be brought together for effective dialogue. The common purpose and the common experience of having played matches together in the past will promote the rich, frank and rewarding discussion that is a necessary basis for co-operative teamwork. In movement activities, a role play or an improvisation can serve as the precursor to a jazz ballet performance: the "feelings" acquired from a vicarious exposure to real life situations will translate into the movement exercises that follow.

Values education

Integrated work in values education and in the Humanities in the senior school seems a wise approach where the syllabus allows it. The Humanities Curriculum Project, as mentioned, is really an exercise in values education. Much of English Literature, too, lends itself to integration with values education through discussion and group work. Although discussion can be the endpoint in values work, a piece of written work, based on the shared ideas of a group of people, is more likely to reflect a wider consideration of values issues than the first and final draft of one isolated mind (Britton, 1970). These ideas spill over into religious studies as well (Self, 1976). A combination of role play, whole class and group discussion preliminary to writing incorporates insights, factual matters and opinions which approaches ignoring oral language work in values education have no chance of matching. Indeed, values education is the heart of the curriculum where oral language activities come together and reinforce one another. Role play can precede discussion; pair work, where children prepare alternative solutions to moral dilemmas, can precede role play. Whole class discussion is enlivened when improvisation work has been used to bring real-life experiences vicariously into the classroom. When values issues can be treated with some objectivity, as when they centre on some historical incident, then even the formal debate is a useful instrument for presenting the case for and against, and for getting inside protagonists.

Summary

Because adolescence is a time when children are beginning to discover and use their capacity for analytical conversation, oral language work provides a key methodology for learning across the senior school curriculum. The acquisition and use of abstract concepts is basic to adolescents' language development and to their capacity to demonstrate their intellectual development. The problem of providing experience-based encounters with the meanings of abstract words is solved through the intellectual demands presented by purposeful discourse.

Oral language work at the senior level, including whole class and group discussion, role play, pair-work, debates and public speaking, can provide the principal method for reaching learning targets. The speed of real learning in most subjects is likely to be increased by talk. Oral language work is the main pedagogy available for promoting a development in children's *analytic competence*, the key acquisition of the upper secondary years.

References

ADLER, M.J. 1983, *How to Speak: How to Listen*. New York: Macmillan.

ALLPORT, D.A. 1983, Language and cognition. In R. HARRIS (ed.), *Approaches to Language*. Oxford: Pergamon Press.

ANASTASIOW, N. 1979, *Oral Language — Expression of Thought*. Urbana, Ill.: ERIC International Reading Association.

ANDERSON, L.M. 1986, *An Oral Language Policy: Friend's Junior School — Kindergarten to Grade Six*. Hobart: Friends' School.

BARNES, D. 1976, *From Communication to Curriculum*. London: Penguin.

BARNES, D., BRITTON, J. & ROSEN, H. 1969, *Language, the Learner and the School*. London: Penguin Education.

BARNES, D., BRITTON, J. & TORBE, M. 1986, *Language, the Learner and the School*. (New Edition) London: Penguin.

BARNES, D. & TODD, F. 1977, *Communication and Learning in Small Groups*. London: Penguin.

BODEN, M.A. 1979, *Piaget*. Glasgow: Fontana.

BOURKE, S.F., CLARK, M.L., DAVIS, D.F. & HOLZER, F. 1980, *Oracy in Australian Schools*. Melbourne: ACER.

BRAUN, C. 1977, Facilitating experience-based language development. In C. BRAUN & V. FROESE (eds), *An Experience-based Approach to Language and Reading*. Baltimore: Uni Park Press.

BREARLEY, M. 1969, *Fundamentals in the First School*. London: Blackwell.

BRITTON, J. 1970, *Language and Learning*. London: Penguin.

BROWN, R. 1959, *Words and Things*. New York: Free Press of Glencoe.

BROWN, G. & YULE, G. 1983 *Discourse Analysis*. Cambridge: Cambridge University Press.

BRUNER, J.S. 1966, *Towards a Theory of Instruction*. London: Harvard University Press.

— 1972, *Relevance of Education*. London: Penguin.

— 1975, Language as an instrument of thought. In A. DAVIES (ed.), *Problems of Language and Learning*. London: Heinemann.

— 1980, *Under Five in Britain* (Oxford Pre-school Research Project). London: Grant McIntyre.

BURNISTON, G. 1968, *Creative Oral Assessment.* Oxford: Pergamon.

CAZDEN, C.B. 1972, *Language in Early Childhood Education.* Washington: National Association for the Education of Young Children.

— 1987, Enhancing teachers' interactions with Maori children in New Zealand. *Language and Education: An International Journal,* 1, 1, 69–71.

CHILVER, P. & GOULD, G. 1982, *Learning and Language in the Classroom.* Oxford: Pergamon Press.

CHOMSKY, N. 1979, *Language and Responsibility.* London: Harvester.

CHRISTIE, F. 1987, Young children's writing: From written to spoken genre, *Language and Education: An International Journal,* 1, 1, 3–13.

CHUKOVSKY, K. 1963, *From Two to Five,* (edited and translated by Miriam Morton). California: University of California Press.

CLAY, M.M. 1985, Engaging with the school system: A study of interactions in the new entrant classroom. *New Zealand Journal of Educational Studies,* 20, 1, 20–38.

CORSON, D.J. 1985, *The Lexical Bar.* Oxford: Pergamon Press.

DALE, P.S. 1976, *Language Development — Structure and Function.* New York: Holt, Rinehart and Winston.

DANNEQUIN, C. 1987, Gagged children: The teaching of French as mother tongue in elementary school. *Language and Education: An International Journal,* 1, 1, 15–31.

DEPARTMENT OF EDUCATION AND SCIENCE 1975, *A Language for Life.* London: Her Majesty's Stationery Office.

DE VILLIERS, J.G. & DE VILLIERS P.A. 1978, *Language Acquisition.* London: Harvard University Press.

DOWNING, J.A. 1969, How children think about reading. *Reading Teacher,* 23, 217–30.

DOWNING, J.A. & THACKRAY, D.V. 1975, *Reading Readiness.* University of London Press.

EDUCATION DEPARTMENT, TASMANIA 1982a, *A School is a Language Place.* Hobart: Education Department.

— 1982b, *Developing a Language Programme.* Hobart: Education Department.

— 1984, *Understanding Reading and Writing.* Hobart: Education Department.

— 1985, *Children, Language and the Arts.* Hobart: Education Department.

EDWARDS, A.D. & FURLONG, V.J. 1978, *The Language of Teaching.* London: Heinemann.

FEAGANS, L. & FARRAN, D. 1982, *The Language of Children Reared in Poverty.* New York: Academic Press.

FILLION, B. 1983, Let me see you learn, *Language Arts*. (September), 702–703.

FLETCHER, P. & GARMAN, M. (eds) 1985, *Language Acquisition*. London: Cambridge University Press.

FREIRE, P. 1972, *Pedagogy of the Oppressed*. London: Penguin.

FRENCH, J. 1985, Whatever happened to language across the curriculum? *Education Canada*. (Winter), 38–43.

FRY. D, 1985, *Children Talk About Books*. Milton Keynes: Open University Press.

GAHAGAN, D.M. & GAHAGAN, D.A. 1971, *Talk Reform — Explorations in Language for Infant School Children*. London: Routledge and Kegan Paul.

GAGNE, R.M. & SMITH, E.C. 1962, A study of the effects of verbalisation on problem solving. *Journal of Experimental Psychology,* 63, 12–18.

GALTON, M.L. 1980, *Inside the Primary Classroom*. London: Routledge and Kegan Paul.

GARVEY, C. 1984, *Children's Talk*. Oxford: Fontana.

GLASS, G.V. *et al.* 1982, *School Class Size: Research and Policy*. Los Angeles: Sage.

GLAZER, S.M. & MORROW, L.M. 1978, The syntactic complexity of primary grade children's oral language and primary reading materials: a comparative analysis. *Journal of Reading Behaviour,* 10, 2.

GOODMAN, K.S. & GOODMAN, Y.M. 1982, Learning about psycholinguistic processes by analyzing oral reading. In F.V. GOLLASCH (ed.), *Language and Literacy: the Selected Writings of Kenneth S. Goodman*. Boston: Routledge and Kegan Paul.

GRAMBS, J.D. & CARR, J.C. 1979, *Modern Methods in Secondary Education*. New York: Holt, Rinehart and Winston.

GRAY, R.A., SASKI, J., MCENTIRE, M.E. & LARSEN, S.C. 1980, Is proficiency in oral language a predictor of academic success? *Elementary School Journal,* 80, 260–68.

HALLIDAY, M.A.K. 1973, *Explorations in the Functions of Language*. London: Arnold.

— 1975, *Learning How to Mean*. London: Arnold.

— 1977, *Explorations in the Development of Language*. New York: Elsevier.

HARVEY, B. 1968, *The Scope of Oracy: Teaching Spoken English*. Oxford: Pergamon.

HENDRICK, J. 1975, *The Whole Child and New Trends in Early Education*. St. Louis: C.V. Mosley.

HIRST, P.H. 1974, *Knowledge and the Curriculum — A Collection of Philosophical Papers*. London: Routledge and Kegan Paul.

HONIG, A.S. 1982, Language environments for young children, *Young Children,* 38:1, 56–67.

HYMES, D. 1972, On communicative competence. In J. PRIDE & J. HOLMES (eds), *Sociolinguistics.* London: Penguin.

LEEPER, S.H. *et al.* 1979, *Good Schools for Young Children.* New York: Macmillan.

LEWIS, R. 1979, Talking in the middle school. *Spoken English,* 12:2, 65–75.

LONGLEY, C. (ed.) 1972, *Games and Simulations.* London: BBC Publications.

LUNZER, E.A. 1968, *The Regulation of Behaviour.* London: Staples.

MACDONALD, B. & WALKER, R. 1976, *Changing the Curriculum.* London: Open Books.

MALLETT, M. & NEWSOME, B. 1977, *Talking, Writing and Learning 8–13.* London: Methuen.

MARKS, M.R. 1951, Problem solving as a function of the situation. *Journal of Experimental Psychology,* 41, 74–80.

MARLAND, M. (ed.) 1977, *Language Across the Curriculum.* London: Heinemann Educational.

MARTIN, N. *et al.* 1976, *Understanding Children Talking.* London: Penguin Educational.

MARTIN, N. 1980, *The Martin Report (What goes on in English Lessons). Case Studies from Government High Schools in Western Australia.* Perth: Department of Education.

MAYBIN, J. 1985, Working towards a school language policy. *Every Child's Language: An In-Service Pack for Primary Teachers.* Clevedon: Multilingual Matters.

MCCARTHY, T. 1984, *The Critical Theory of Jurgen Habermas.* Cambridge: Polity Press.

MENYUK, P. 1977, *The Acquisition and Development of Language.* New York: Prentice Hall.

MILLS, R.W. (ed.) 1977, *Teaching English Across the Ability Range.* London: Ward Lock.

MINISTRY OF EDUCATION 1963, *Half Our Future.* London: Her Majesty's Stationery Office.

MOFFETT, J. 1968, *Teaching the Universe of Discourse.* London: Houghton Mifflin.

MOON, C. & WELLS, G. 1979, The influence of home on learning to read. *Journal of Research in Reading.* (Leeds) 2, 53–62.

NATIONAL ASSOCIATION FOR THE TEACHING OF ENGLISH. 1976, *Language Across the Curriculum: Guidelines for Schools.* Birmingham: Ward Lock.

ONTARIO MINISTRY OF EDUCATION 1984, *Ontario Schools: Intermediate and Senior Divisions*. Toronto: Ministry of Education.

PALMER, J.O. 1964, A restandardisation of adolescent norms for the Shipley Hartford. *Journal of Clinical Psychology,* 20, 492–95.

PARSONS, B. *et al.* 1984, *Drama, Language and Learning*. Hobart: National Association for Drama in Education.

PEEL, E.A. & DE SILVA, W.A. 1972, Some aspects of higher level learning processes during adolescence. In W.D. WALL & D.P. VARMA (eds), *Advances in Educational Psychology*. London: University of London Press.

PETERS, R.S. 1967, *The Concept of Education*. London: Routledge and Kegan Paul.

PHILLIPS, G.M. *et al.* 1970, *The Development of Oral Communication in the Classroom*. New York: Bobbs Merrill.

PIAGET, J. 1978, *The Development of Thought: Equilibration and Cognitive Structures*. London: Blackwell.

PIAGET, J. & INHELDER, B. 1958, *The Growth of Logical Thinking: From Childhood to Adolescence*. London: Routledge and Kegan Paul.

POPPER, K.R. 1972, *Objective Knowledge: An Evolutionary Approach*. Oxford: Clarendon.

POPPER, K.R. & ECCLES, J.C. 1977, *The Self and its Brain*. Berlin: Springer International.

REED, J.E. 1976, Oral language teaching in the primary school. Unpublished MA dissertation. Dept. of Curriculum Studies, University of London, Institute of Education.

REID, J.F. 1966, Learning to think about reading. *Educational Research,* 9, 56–62.

ROBERTS, G.R. 1972, *English in Primary Schools*. London: Routledge and Kegan Paul.

ROBINSON, W.P. 1978, *Language Management in Education — The Australian Context*. London: Allen and Unwin.

ROBINSON, W.P. (ed.), 1981, *Communication in Development*. London: Academic Press.

ROMAINE, S. 1984, *The Language of Children and Adolescents: The Acquisition of Communicative Competence*. London: Blackwell.

ROSEN, C. & ROSEN, H. 1973, *The Language of Primary School Children*. London: Penguin.

ROSENTHAL, R. & JACOBSON, L. 1968, *Pygmalion in the Classroom,* New York: Holt, Rinehart and Winston.

SCHOOLS COUNCIL WORKING PAPER 64, 1979, *Learning through Talking 11–16*. London: Methuen.

— 67, 1980, *Language Across the Curriculum*. London: Methuen.

SELF, D. 1976, *Talk — a practical guide.* London: Ward Lock.

SIEGAL, M. 1975, Spontaneous development of moral concepts. *Human Development,* 18, 370–83.

STEINER, G. 1978, *On Difficulty and Other Essays.* Oxford University Press.

STRINGER, L. 1977, Drama games and simulation. In R.W. MILLS (ed.), *Teaching English Across the Ability Range.* London: Ward Lock.

TIZARD, B. & HUGHES, M. 1984, *Young Children Learning: Talking and Thinking at Home and at School.* London: Fontana

TORBE, M. 1980, *Language Policies in Action.* London: Ward Lock.

TOUGH, J. 1977, *Talking and Learning.* London: Ward Lock.

— 1979, *Talk for Teaching and Learning.* London: Ward Lock.

VERMA, G.K. & BAGLEY, C. 1975, *Race and Education Across Cultures.* London: Heinemann.

VERNON, M.D. 1957, *Backwardness in Reading.* London: Cambridge University Press.

VYGOTSKY, L.S. 1962, *Thought and Language.* Cambridge, Mass.: MIT Press.

WARDHAUGH, R. 1985, *How Conversation Works.* Oxford: Blackwell.

WAY, B. 1967, *Development through Drama.* London: Longmans.

WELLS, C.G. 1974, Learning to code experience through language. *Journal of Child Language.* 1, 243–69.

— 1984, *Language Development in the Pre-School Years.* London: Cambridge University Press.

WILKINSON, A. 1965, *Spoken English.* University of Birmingham Press.

— 1977, *The Foundations of Language,* Oxford: Oxford University Press.

WOOD, D., MCMAHON, L. & CRANSTOUN, Y. 1980, *Working with Under Fives.* London: Grant McIntyre.

YOUNG, M.F.D. (ed.) 1971, *Knowledge and Control — New Directions for the Sociology of Education.* London: Collier-MacMillan.

Index